A Sound Mind

A Sound Mind

*Christian principles for mental health
through a God-governed thought life*

David Matthew

Leaf Publishing

Leaf Publishing
England
www.leafpublishing.co.uk

Scripture quotations are normally taken from the NIV—the Holy Bible, New International Version. Copyright © 1973, 1978,1984 by International Bible Society. Used by permission of Hodder & Stoughton Limited.

ISBN 0-9552274-0-2

The original edition of this work was published by Harvestime in 1987 under the same title. This updated and expanded edition is published by Leaf Publishing 2006.

Published by Leaf Publishing
www.leafpublishing.co.uk

Contents

To Rachel: sound in mind and sweet in nature

Note: While this book is written primarily for committed Christian readers, many of the principles it sets out are valid for everyone. An Appendix at the end of the book sets out what it means to be a Christian.

Introduction

But for the grace of God I would long since have been in a mental institution.

From childhood, something inside me instinctively knew there must be some bedrock truths to support a steady existence, some solid convictions to live by. But humanistic schoolteachers, poets, novelists and scientists combined to impress upon me, from the age of five onwards, that life was fundamentally meaningless.

As I grew older my mind became a battleground. How could the supposed virtue of an open mind be reconciled with the firm convictions of Christian faith?

As the two ideologies fought for control of my thinking, I would incline towards first one, then the other. To yield my mind to God would be to restrict its activity. Surely that couldn't be right? Yet to embrace the teaching of humanism would be to suffer like Phyllis McGinley, who wrote:

> *Ah, snug lie those that slumber*
> *Beneath Conviction's roof.*
> *Their floors are sturdy lumber,*
> *Their windows weatherproof.*
> *But I sleep cold forever*
> *And cold sleep all my kind,*
> *For I was born to shiver*
> *In the draft from an open mind.*

That 'draft from an open mind' has smitten modern man

with a mental pneumonia from which he is slowly dying. Psychiatric wards and mental institutions are full of the terminally sick in mind.

For myself, I wanted to live—to the full. That very quality of life, I discovered, was what Jesus promised (John 10:10), but at a price: I would have to submit my whole being—*my mind included*—to his rule. The grace of God prevailed. The Lord God of Armies won the battle for my mind and I became a Christian.

Once committed to Jesus, I discovered that my thought processes needed re-educating, that a 'renewing of the mind' was required. Far from being a one-off crisis, this turned out to be a lifelong process, one I have been happily involved in now for over fifty years.

To my delight I have discovered that true mental freedom lies, not in keeping an open mind and doing one's own thing, but in having the right master. Jesus has proved to be that right Master.

In this book I share some of the liberating insights that the Lord has given me as part of the mind-renewing process. May they prove equally liberating to you.

David Matthew
Castleford, England, 2006

Chapter 1

A sound mind

'Suicide while the balance of his mind was disturbed.'

You put down the newspaper with a sigh. Another tragic end to a human life, the file closed with the coroner's blunt verdict.

A host of questions flood into your head as you sip your coffee with a faraway look in your eye and ponder that grim phrase: 'While the balance of his mind was disturbed'. What fearful mental tortures racked the victim before the event? What dark forces dominated his thinking? How could anyone, you ask yourself, sink so low in depression and despair as to take his own life?

Then the most fearful question of all: could it ever happen to you?

With a shudder, you dismiss the haunting prospect from your mind and busy yourself with the day's work. Some things are best not even contemplated!

Nevertheless, while most people manage to stay on the right side of insanity, and of suicide, we all have to admit that mental pressures can sometimes be intense. The human mind is such a delicate instrument; its fine balance is liable to be upset by a variety of factors.

Let's consider some of them.

Health and temperament

There's our *physical health* or lack of it. We are often negative here. A thumping headache is quick to convince us that we are suffering from a brain tumour. Or a twinge of pain in the chest triggers off a train of thought that within seconds has us visualising our own funeral, complete with hearse, graveside committal and weeping relatives.

Then there are *hereditary factors.* 'How I wish I hadn't been born so intelligent!' a student once complained to me. 'If only I could have been the average type who's content to amble through life, satisfied with a routine job, a bit of gardening at weekends and a few pints of beer with some friends down at the pub. But as it is, I've inherited a keen brain. I find myself asking deeper questions about life. The trouble is, the answers don't come easily, and when they do come they're nearly always depressing.'

While there is truth in the proverb, 'When ignorance is bliss 'tis folly to be wise', the fact remains that, in practice, we often have little choice. We have to cope with what we are—a sharp mind included.

Temperament is another part of our hereditary makeup. We have all met the 'artistic' type who is highly sensitive to mood and atmosphere. His permanent state seems to be mildly manic-depressive—one minute he is on a guffawing, backslapping 'high', the next in the pit of despair. He is just made that way.

Similar to him is the introverted thinker, categorised by the ancients as 'melancholic'. He is the 'dark horse', the 'strong, silent type' who thinks a great deal but says little. He ponders deep issues till his mind comes near to bursting point, because the longer he ponders, the more convinced he becomes that there are no satisfying answers. When the melancholic sees a poster bearing the legend: 'Sometimes I sit and think, and sometimes I just sit', he lets out a sigh and wishes with all his heart that he could escape out of the first situation into the second. But he knows he can't.

Closely allied to heredity are *emotional factors*. Generally speaking, a woman's mind is more prone to be influenced by these than a man's. Often there is a glandular or hormonal aspect, as is commonly the case with pre-menstrual tension, post-natal depression and the menopause.

Age, too, has a bearing on our state of mind. Mental sharpness tends to be dulled with the advancing years. Memory begins to fail. We become less able to cope with a variety of demands at the same time. Sometimes confusion sets in and, especially for those unable to get out and about, the ability to distinguish past and present events slips away as time seems to stand still.

Yet another element is *use.* Just as an arm or leg muscle will atrophy from lack of use, so will the 'muscles' of the mind. Conversely, a mind kept active by new challenges and a variety of stimuli tends to remain fitter for longer. Apparently older folk who do crosswords or sudoku, or even play bingo, are more liable to enjoy robust mental health.

Over and above these factors governing our mental condition, however, there are others peculiar to the times in which we live.

Pressures of today's world

We are all *world-conscious* in a way unknown to any previous generation. Living, as we do, in the era of computers, television and long-haul air travel, we are robbed of the parochial view of life common to our ancestors.

TV is here to stay, whether we like it or not. Thanks to satellite communications and videophones, reports of earthquakes, wars, famines, revolutions and disasters are pumped into our sitting-rooms from 'embedded reporters' right as they happen, complete with moving, talking pictures in full colour. One viewer was heard to comment, 'I don't know which is the worse: watching the early evening news and being too frightened to eat my meal, or watching the late night news and being unable to sleep.'

Yes, world-consciousness can be a mental burden. The often-heard remark, 'What on earth is the world coming to?', is a comment peculiarly appropriate to our times.

Even more difficult to cope with is the *accelerating rate of change*. Time was when life was ninety per cent predictable. The routines of youth, marriage, family life, employment, retirement and death varied little from one generation to the next. Like a marathon runner who has reconnoitred the course, people used to be able to pace themselves through life with a fair degree of certainty. For our generation such a luxury has gone for ever. Life is so unpredictable, so full of change and uncertainty that it could better be likened to a commando being parachuted into enemy territory. Anything can happen!

My grandmother remembered the motor-car being invented. Now we can fly in cushioned comfort at 500 miles per hour, seven miles up, relishing a gourmet meal to the sound of stereo music before watching the in-flight movie. More than that, we have men on the moon and space probes taking close-up photos of distant planets.

Previous generations wrote books long-hand or, more recently, with a typewriter. I'm writing this, of course, on a computer screen using a word-processor, juggling words and sentences around at the touch of a button. At the touch of another button the whole book is captured in seconds onto the disk and a backup copy saved at a safe location elsewhere. Yet another touch will set the printer purring away to produce an effortless printout. All very normal, yet I have seen older writers peer at my computer with a wary expression. To them it represents the unknown, and the unknown is frightening. Technology, though potentially so helpful, can also be scary— a pressure on the mind because it represents change and the end of the already short-lived status quo.

Added to this uncertainty is a related and equally heavy, pressure: *the frantic pace of modern life.*

While the 'hurry factor' varies, we're all caught up in it to some extent. Being in a frantic hurry is seen at its worst in the big-city commuter waiting on the station platform for the early train into town. He glances nervously at his watch. The train is thirty seconds overdue! His body stiffens with impatience; his heart rate increases; with knuckles white from tension he taps his foot on the ground, as if to send a morse message to urge the train on. He breaks into a cold sweat as his mind races ahead to possible missed connections in town, work-time lost and a host of other upsets to his over-busy, over-scheduled life.

For many in the western world, *economic uncertainty* adds to the mental burden. While the pressure to possess material things increases, the means to buy them become, for many, less readily available. They find themselves gripped in the tight coils of the credit system or stabbed in the back by their 'flexible friend', the credit card. Adjustable interest rates, short job-contracts, pension problems, rocketing fuel prices or the threat of unemployment combine to make financial planning ever more difficult.

And in some of the nations with a now-forsaken Christian heritage, *increasing lawlessness,* either real or perceived, constitutes a growing pressure on the mind of 'the man in the street'. More and more he is becoming 'the man indoors', for the street is a dangerous place to be, especially after dark, in spite of anti-social behaviour orders on local yobs.

For a few, these pressures are compounded by *physiological factors.* A chemical imbalance or glandular malfunction can affect the mind in a big way, turning a person with a well-integrated personality into someone who crouches weeping in a corner, unable to grasp what is happening.

Little wonder, then, that under such a barrage of pressure the mind of modern man is prone to disintegrate. 'I'm nearly out of my mind with worry' is all too commonplace a remark. And, for some, the mental burden becomes too much. No longer able to maintain the equilibrium of their mind, they end up the subject of yet another coroner's report.

The believer's birthright

What about you? Can you reasonably expect to stay sane under present conditions?

If you are not a Christian in the Bible sense of the word—see the Appendix to this book if you are unclear what that means—there can be no guarantees. But for the believer in Jesus Christ, filled with the Holy Spirit, the prospects are altogether brighter. Mental stability, however, does not come from dodging the pressures. Becoming a hermit isn't the answer. Nowhere in Scripture does God promise his followers a smooth ride. As long as you live in the same world as every-one else you will have to face the same pressures. But your happy privilege as a Christian is to experience power sufficient to keep you sane and mentally healthy in the very midst of the pressures. Your birthright in Christ includes *a sound mind!*

You may need to adjust your thinking a little if you were raised on the notion that Christ 'saves souls'. He doesn't just save souls in the sense of the intangible, immaterial part of us, scorning interest in our bodies or our brains. No, he saves the whole person, body and mind included. And while it is true that we shall have to wait until the age to come to enjoy the fulness of our redemption, we can still enjoy a substantial taste of that age's powers right here and now.

'God has not given us a spirit of fear, but of power and of love and of *a sound mind'*.[1] The apostle Paul's statement is true for *you* and for *now!*

Don't worry if your version of the Bible translates 'a sound mind' as 'discipline' or 'self-discipline'. That's because the original Greek has no exact English equivalent and several different ideas comprise its overall meaning. The *Amplified Bible* wraps it all up in a tidy package as follows: 'He has given us a spirit of power and of love and of calm and well-balanced mind and discipline and self-control.'

Here, in fact, we have the same Greek word used to describe the once-suicidal maniac named Legion. After Jesus had dealt with the demonic powers that governed his life, the man was found by the astonished locals 'sitting there, dressed and *in his right mind'*.[2] Jesus simply restored him to normality. The touch of Jesus upon a human life always has that effect. He brings order out of chaos. He stills the mental storm to produce in the human mind 'a great calm'.

Has he touched you with his salvation? If so, then a sound mind is your privilege. If not, now is the time to step out of the driving seat of your life and hand over the controls to him.

A mind 'held together'

It is one thing to receive a sound mind at the touch of the Lord. It is another thing to hold on to it. Many a tormented mind, initially stilled at the divine command, has in time become turbulent again.

In no way can we lay the blame on the Lord; he always does a reliable job. The problem lies in our failure to live in the good of what he has done. And why does that happen? Chiefly because we don't understand what the Scripture teaches about the mind. If we ignore the Maker's guidelines for the *maintenance* of mental health it should come as no surprise to find the machinery running into difficulties. Together, therefore, we're going to explore some of the Bible's principles for mental health and stability.

Do you find yourself right now in a state of mental turmoil? Does your mind feel as if it must break apart any moment? I understand; I've been there. I pray that the Lord himself will give you sufficient calm and concentration to stay alert as we look into his Word together.

Paul said about Christ: 'In him all things hold together'.[3] 'All things' includes *your mind*. Jesus can hold your mind together. Trust him to do it while you read through these pages. By the time you have finished you will be in a position to co-operate with him to make it a permanent arrangement.

Chapter 1 NOTES

[1] 2 Timothy 1:7 NKJV

[2] Mark 5:15

[3] Colossians 1:17

Chapter 2

Mind dethroned

It begins in the primary school classroom—a brain-washing process that teaches us to accept without question that Mind is king.

Our thoughts, we are told, can wander unchallenged, like sacred cows in India, wherever they will; nothing and no-one has the right to forbid them passage. There is no higher authority.

By the time we reach our teenage years, the indoctrination has bitten deep, to the point where most of us don't even realise that there could be an alternative to Mind as king. Were someone to voice the possibility our likely response would be: 'What do you mean? How can my mind *not* be its own boss? Surely no-one else can legislate for what goes on inside my head!'

But we would be wrong. *God* claims ultimate rule. His is the authority over all things, and 'all things' includes our thinking.

A bit of history

Down the centuries God's claim has been disputed. Not only have individuals asserted the independence of their own minds, but some have also attempted to dictate the thinking of others. The ancient pagan priests attempted this, and largely succeeded. They asserted their rule over the minds and consciences of those they purported to serve, uttering dire threats over any person daring to think independently. Today this usurping of God's authority still goes on. Witch-doctors, dictators and cult leaders the world over keep a tight grip on the reins of people's thinking.

Historically, it was probably the Greeks who first broke free, declaring, 'No-one must be allowed to tell us what to think or believe. No limits must be set on human thought. Everything must be open to examination, everything called into question.' In general, however, thinking in Europe continued to develop through the Middle Ages along Christian lines (using 'Christian' in its broadest sense), with God acknowledged by all and his right to make demands on their minds implicitly accepted. Not until the eighteenth century was that situation overturned.

Rationalism: the rule of mind

In that century, in the trend known as *rationalism*, human reason finally exalted itself above God. 'Start by doubting everything—even God's existence' became the watchword. Philosophers and thinkers began to kick against the rule of God and Christ, shouting, 'Let us break their chains...and throw off their fetters'.[1]

In France at this time—the period of the French Revolution—the liberation of the mind from the supposed shackles of God found expression in the setting up of the Goddess of Reason in the heart of the nation's institutional church, the cathedral of Notre Dame in Paris.

As the ideas of the philosophers spread through European society more widely, Reason tightened its hold on the throne. It became ever more bold in its claim to absolute rule, and few dared challenge that claim. The belief soon prevailed, as it still does, that the human mind could even analyse God. How foolish! Man can no more fathom the mysteries of God with his little brain than he can suck the ocean dry with a drinking-straw. Pascal was right in observing that 'the last function of reason is to recognise that there are an infinity of things which surpass it'.

Today we live as the heirs of western rationalism. But there is one difference. Whereas in the eighteenth century the supremacy of the mind was the philosophy of a few professional thinkers (like Berkeley, Hume, Voltaire and Rousseau) and of their educated disciples, now it has filtered down to the grassroots of society. Today we all regard it as self-evident that we can think what we want to think. Mind is worshipped universally—even in the primary school classroom.

The Christian difference

But we who are Christians cannot fall into line. We break out of our generation's cultural straitjacket by declaring that God alone rules all things, even our minds. Convinced that if he isn't Lord of all, he isn't Lord at all, we tell him, *'Lord, we concede your right to govern our thought-life.'*

This must be our starting point in considering the whole question of the human mind. The Bible underlines it as the number one priority by declaring, 'The fear of the Lord is the beginning of knowledge'.[2] We could add that the fear of the Lord—that is, the according to him of his rightful place as ruler—is also the first step to mental stability.

To exalt your own mind to kingship is to load it with a weight of responsibility that it is ill-equipped to carry. As major questions about life, death, purpose and direction arrive in a steady stream on its desk, requiring decisions, it begins to panic. It lacks the capacity for making such taxing decisions. Soon, it begins to crack under the strain.

But God can never be overloaded. It is no burden at all to him that the buck stops at his desk. You can therefore submit to God with confidence and, in so doing, release your mind from unbearable pressure.

Your mind under the Word

So far so good. But what does it mean, in practice, to bow to God? First of all it means *submitting your mind to God's Word— the Bible.*

Take, for example, the question of where the universe came from. Astronomers and scholars have put forward a variety of suggestions: the Continuous Expansion theory, the Steady State theory, the Big Bang theory. What do we believe? Genesis presents us with an account of the direct creation of the universe by God, an account summarised by Hebrews 11:3 in the neat statement: 'By faith we understand that the universe was formed at God's command, so that what is seen was not made out of what was visible.'

There you have it: *'By faith we understand'.*

Faith is simply taking God at his word. When he declares, 'I personally spoke the universe into being', you submit your mind to his word and so find true understanding. You are not free to consider alternatives. At last you know the answer to a question that has baffled the minds of eggheads for as long as humanity has existed.

Bigger questions than this also have their answer in God's Word:

- Why are you here? Because God willed it.

- What is the purpose of your life? To know God and to co-operate with him in his eternal plan.

- What does death hold for you, as a Christian? Being with Christ, which is far better than anything experienced this side of the grave or the crematorium furnace.

- Do you have any real significance? Yes, you are a unique expression of God, chosen by him, supported by him, loved by him.

Smile, God loves you!

What joy and comfort we find in submitting our minds to such glorious truths! What cause for godly hilarity! And what a far cry from the plight of the Earl of Chesterfield, an eighteenth-century thinker, who glumly remarked, 'Since attaining the full use of my reason no-one has ever heard me laugh.'

Indeed, there is little cause for joy or laughter in what King Reason offers his subjects. The universe, he says, is a chance collocation of atoms, a happening without purpose. You, too, are without purpose—you have no significance, no hope and no meaningful expectations either this side of death or beyond. According to King Reason, you are a feeble swimmer in a vast, endless sea, with no rescue vessel in sight. You are destined to struggle to keep your head above water until your puny strength runs out and you sink to a frightening, meaningless end.

Give me God's way any time!

Have *you* broken free from the tyranny of the mind? Five centuries ago, a German monk named Martin Luther broke free from another tyranny: the mental and spiritual bondage imposed by a corrupt Church. Today's religion is a different one: humanism, with its idolising of the mind. It's our privilege, as it was Luther's, to break free and gladly embrace a new captivity, declaring as he did, 'My conscience is taken captive by God's Word. On this I take my stand. I can do no other. God help me. Amen.'

Your mind under the Spirit

Second, to bow to God means *submitting your mind to the Holy Spirit within you.*

The Holy Spirit *is* God. He will show you things that the unaided human mind can never grasp, things that God alone can make known.[3] To begin with, he will bring assurance of salvation, convincing you beyond doubt that you are indeed God's beloved child.

I knew a young woman who was born again, baptised as a believer and filled with the Holy Spirit. As a result, her life was transformed. Her rationalistic husband, however, had no time for such 'religious nonsense'. Determined to rid his wife of her Christian fantasies, he patiently explained to her how God couldn't possibly exist and how her so-called new birth was no more than an emotional 'high'.

She listened dutifully to all his persuasive arguments. When he had finished, she flashed him a winning smile and said, 'Well, thank you for all your reasoning, dear. I certainly can't answer your arguments, but I just *know* I'm a child of God, and my sins are forgiven and...oh, it's so wonderful!'

The poor man nearly tore his hair out! His mental gymnastics were no match for the conviction of a mind persuaded by God's Holy Spirit.

Anointed to know

'You have an anointing from the Holy One, and all of you
know the truth,' explains John.[4] He makes a connection
between being anointed with the Holy Spirit and knowing the
truth.

The 'truth' he refers to here is more than doctrinal ortho-
doxy. It is the kind of everyday truth that we require in the
most ordinary of circumstances. John is saying that the presence of the Holy Spirit will, among other things, guide you
when your natural mind is in a dilemma, enabling you to
reach a sound decision.

Among a class of seventeen-year-old girls the major topic
of conversation one day was a popular novel that had won
notoriety for its strong element of perverted sex. Jenny, a
Christian, didn't read it; she knew that such a book would do
her thought-life no good.

'Hey, Jenny, what do *you* think of this book?' queried one
of her friends.

'Oh, I've no time for it.'

'So you've read it, then?'

'No.'

'What! Well how on earth can you pronounce judgment
on something you haven't even read?'

'Well, for a start, its reputation's bad enough. But, apart
from that, I just know inside myself that it would foul up my
mind. So I've chosen to give it a miss.'

'That's stupid!'

'Maybe it is to you, but to me it makes good sense.'

A Christian like Jenny—or you—doesn't need to test

everything with the mind. That's the world's way: 'Mind is boss, so let it make all the decisions.' The Holy Spirit will sometimes lead you to wise decisions directly, when to involve your powers of mental analysis would stain your mind with moral dirt. It's not just books. Some newspapers, movies, magazines and websites can be equally harmful.

'I want you to be wise about what is good,' urged Paul, *'and innocent about what is evil'.*[5] Let your mind range freely around matters that are wholesome and good. That's wisdom. But when you hear alarm bells ringing at a deeper level than the mind—in the depths of your spirit—choose to turn your mind away. Don't watch that film or leaf through that magazine. To adapt the motto of a popular brand: 'Just don't do it!'

Bankrupt logic

Moral questions apart, man's powers of logic are simply inadequate to handle *any* spiritual truth. Paul once came across a classic example in some people in Rome who argued like this:

> 'Sin is a sad fact of life. But, happily, God's grace reaches out to deal with it. The more sin there is, the more of God's grace flows out. The grace of God is a wonderful thing; we can never get too much of it. Why, then, don't we sin as much as we can, so that more and more of God's wonderful grace will be drawn out in response?'

Now that is perfectly logical by the standards of human reason, but by God's reckoning it is perfectly wrong. Paul didn't even consider it worth arguing over; he just dismissed it out of hand.[6] In the end, true understanding in such cases comes, not by logic, which may be spiritually questionable, but by revelation from the Holy Spirit of God, who takes one look at the world's wisdom and sticks a warning label on it: 'Foolishness'.[7]

In the light of all this, then, *your first step to mental stability is to dethrone your mind and acknowledge the rule of God.* Your mind makes a good servant but a bad master. Let your thinking, therefore, renounce its claim to independence and agree to be restricted by God's Word and God's Spirit.

Happy restriction

'Restricted?' you reply. 'That sounds like intellectual suicide. Surely restriction is a bad thing, isn't it?'

Not necessarily. In fact, some restrictions are altogether good. A train, for instance, runs far better when it is restricted to the rails. A football match makes sense only if the players restrict themselves to the rules. Traffic flows smoothly only when it is restricted to the correct side of the road. And your mind will operate successfully only when it is restricted to the guidelines of God.

Are you willing to submit your mind to his rule? The rest of this book assumes that you are.

If you have already done so, the basic issue is settled. You may, however, be struggling with making this mental submission a moment-by-moment reality. In spite of your best efforts, stray thoughts keep breaking away from the herd and heading off on their own. So what do you do?

We shall look at this in detail later on, but for the time being let the apostle Paul provide the answer. 'We take captive every thought,' he says, 'to make it obedient to Christ'.[8] So ride out after those stray thoughts. Rope them in and haul them back to Christ's corral.

Let this become a way of life. Insist that *every* thought submit to the Lord, to his Word and to his Spirit. That is true freedom.

Chapter 2 NOTES

[1] Psalm 2:2-3

[2] Proverbs 1:7

[3] See 1 Corinthians 2:9-12

[4] 1 John 2:20

[5] Romans 16:19

[6] See Romans 6:1-2

[7] 1 Corinthians 3:19

[8] 2 Corinthians 10:5

Chapter 3

You're responsible

God has a habit of returning to us as a stewardship the gifts we give him.

Abraham, knife in hand, received Isaac back from the altar of sacrifice. Jochebed set baby Moses afloat on the Nile, entrusting him to the care of God, who promptly returned him to her by way of Pharaoh's daughter. He does the same with your mind. You submit your thinking to God only to find that he hands it back, saying, 'Look after this for me.'

What a responsibility!

'Lord,' you gasp, 'this is my *mind* we're talking about! It's a highly sensitive and powerful instrument. In fact it's potentially explosive. I'm not sure I have the ability to handle it properly.'

His response? 'You can do it, child.'

When my children were small, I didn't allow them much liberty because they lacked the experience and wisdom to handle it. I made most decisions for them. 'Daddy, can I have a piece of chocolate, please?' would prompt answers like, 'Yes, but be sure to take off all the silver paper first' or, 'No, you've just cleaned your teeth for bedtime.' At seventeen, however, my son found me taking a different approach. 'Dad, how would you feel about my going to an all-night disco?' would prompt a few observations ending with, 'But the final decision must be yours, son.' He knew my general feelings on such issues. Better still, as an active Christian himself, he could make wise judgments based on his own walk with the Lord.

This is the way God treats you and me—as adults, not as children. He credits us with enough spiritual sense, indwelt by the Holy Spirit as we are, to handle our own thinking wisely. He trusts us to think about the right things.

The choice is yours

'Think about the right things?' you retort. 'Are you suggesting I can *choose* what I think about?'

Exactly.

'That's a pretty radical statement!'

Radical it is—but true. In fact, you not only *can* but *must* choose what you think about. You gave your thinking to God and he has now returned it with the message: 'Look after it for me, please. I know you can do it.'

Statements like this, that cut across common assumptions, need biblical support if we are to believe them. Such support is not lacking when it comes to our ability to govern our own thoughts. For now, consider just a couple of the apostle Paul's statements. First: 'Whatever is true, whatever is noble, whatever is right, whatever is pure, whatever is lovely, whatever is admirable—if anything is excellent or praiseworthy—*think about such things*'.[1] That is no mere hint, or the expression of a vain hope—'It would be great if you could ever manage it'. It's a command.

What's the point of giving commands if obedience is impossible? The very fact that Scripture *commands* you to think about certain things takes for granted your ability to do so, with God's help. When Jesus encountered the man with the withered hand he commanded him to do the one thing that, unaided, he could not do: 'Stretch out your hand.' Along with the command came the divine enabling and the account records: 'So he stretched it out and it was completely restored'.[2] With God's help you *can* 'think about such things'.

Again: *'Set your minds* on things above,' says Paul, 'not on earthly things'.[3] You can choose what to set your mind on, so go on—set it on good, wholesome 'heavenly' topics. Think godly thoughts.

'Nice idea,' you respond, 'but it just doesn't work like that. Sometimes I find my mind filled with all sorts of garbage. It just appears. Sad, but that's how it is. I suppose I'm just not a very good Christian yet. One of these days, maybe, all those beautiful thoughts that Paul wrote about will start coming into my mind, but for the time being I seem to be at the mercy of rubbishy thinking.'

Rest assured, you are normal. We all find the most appalling thoughts entering our minds unbidden. Sometimes it happens in our most holy moments—when sharing our faith with someone, while taking the bread and wine of Communion or in the middle of a time of prayer or worship. They may be violent, lustful, proud or spiteful thoughts and we feel deeply ashamed.

It is vital to understand one thing: to have such thoughts is not sin. You don't (I hope) invite them in. You certainly don't *want* them in. They just appear. So don't let the devil convince you you're a terrible sinner on that score. You are not. It is no sin to be tempted; sin is *yielding* to temptation. The big issue is not *whether* unhelpful thoughts enter your mind—they do— but *what you do with them when you find them.* And that responsibility, remember, is given by God to you. As Martin Luther wisely observed: you can't stop the birds landing on your head, but you can stop them making a nest in your hair.

Dealing with gate-crashers

Look at it this way. You have been out shopping and on your return discover, to your alarm, that the house door is ajar. You distinctly remember locking it when you went out; someone must have forced an entry.

You creep down the hallway. Strange voices are coming from the lounge. Slowly, you peer round the door to see three filthy vagrants in there. One is stuffing your CD collection into a bag; the other two are spitting on the floor and laughing as they lie back on your best sofa with their muddy feet up on the polished mahogany coffee-table. What a nerve!

In you burst. You have two possible courses of action. One is to say, 'Make yourselves comfortable, boys. Tea or coffee? And while I'm making it, do help yourself to the family silver.' The other is to show them the door. It's your house, after all; they came in uninvited and you have every right to kick them out.

Thoughts gatecrash your mind that way. You suddenly discover them there, uninvited, unexpected and unclean. Whether you entertain them or throw them out is entirely up to you.

Of course, not all gate-crashing thoughts are dirty, selfish or violent. They may just as likely be from God, ones that are wholesome and good, in which case it is to your advantage to invite them to stay around. But the others: order them out.

Look at it another way: your mind is like the airspace over

a country's national boundary. Aircraft keep flying in from neighbouring countries. Some are friendly and are allowed to land; others may be enemy aircraft intent on destruction. These are met with opposition from the national air force, to be either turned away or destroyed.

And who is in the control tower? You are. You have the ability to grant or refuse those thoughts entry permission, to smooth the way for a landing or to call out the fighters.

How to test intruders

Obviously, if the Lord holds you responsible for your own thoughts he must provide you with the equipment to test each one. What touchstone, then, does he provide?

He provides his *Word.* Thoughts that contradict the wholesome teaching of the Bible need throwing out right away. Lurid sexual fantasies, for example, hardly come in any of the categories listed by Paul in the verse quoted above. So order them out. A sudden impulse to pocket the gold watch that someone has left in the factory washroom is anti-scriptural, too,[4] so reject it.

God also provides the touchstone of his *Holy Spirit.* As a Spirit-filled believer, you instinctively know a thought's origin.

Suppose you are riding your motorcycle down a lane towards a crossroads. Buildings at either side of the junction prevent you from seeing what traffic is coming along the major road until you get right up to the junction. As you approach it, the thought suddenly enters your head to drive straight across without stopping and gamble on nothing crossing your path.

Not only does such an impulse conflict with common-sense safety precautions, but the Holy Spirit within you will tell you right away that it comes straight from the devil, who is a murderer.[5] So reject it. Slow down at the junction, look both ways and drive across only when it is safe to do so.

Or you are walking down the High Street when a young mother walks by with a toddler in a pushchair. You suddenly find in your mind a strong impulse to pray silently for the child, that God will bless him and keep him from evil. That is hardly a devilish impulse. It is from the Lord, so act on it.

Other thoughts may not be as easily identified. Suppose, for example, you are lying in bed and the words of the song *Tie a Yellow Ribbon* keep going round and round in your head. You probably heard someone singing or whistling it during the day and it has stuck, repeating like a hiccupy CD. What do you do? How do you test this one?

Ask yourself some basic questions. Is it blessing you? No. Is it that the words are blatantly evil? No, they're harmless enough. Is it a persistent nuisance? Yes, that's it. You can't get the song out of your mind and it is driving you crazy.

Now God is a God of peace.[6] He wants your mind to be dwelling on constructive things, not on endless repetitions of *Tie a Yellow Ribbon.* The Holy Spirit makes it clear that this is just another enemy tactic—sending a few light aircraft buzzing in and out across the borders of your mind as a form of harassment, keeping you on edge so that you get no rest. Recognise these thoughts for what they are, then, and send them packing.

Like any new skill, checking out your thoughts improves with practice. The Bible defines the spiritually mature as those 'who by *constant use* have trained themselves to distinguish good from evil'.[7] Better start practising right away.

Immigration controls

It goes without saying that the whole process becomes futile if you don't watch the entry points of your mind. Computer enthusiasts will know the expressive term *gigo,* which stands for 'garbage in, garbage out'. In other words, if you type the wrong key-strokes into the computer, you can't expect it to turn out anything but mistakes.

Your mind works on exactly the same basis. Watch the company you keep, the books and newspapers you read, the TV programmes you watch, the talk and music you listen to. Your authority to throw out any intruding vagrants is severely undermined if they can legitimately turn around and say, 'Wait a minute, it was you who invited us in.'

The *gigo* principle works in reverse, too. Opening your mind and senses to good and wholesome material can only trigger good and wholesome thoughts.

Again, the choice is yours. When exposure to garbage is beyond your control to prevent, you can look confidently to the Lord for help—for example, when your workmates constantly use bad language or decorate their wall-space with sexy posters. But, for the most part, you can choose what enters your mind through the gates of your senses. The exercise of strict immigration controls at the entry points to your mind is your own responsibility. Don't ask God to do for you what he expects you to do for yourself.

More about this in the next chapter. Meanwhile, grasp the vital truth we have outlined here: that you yourself are responsible. You are responsible on two counts. First, to guard the entry points to your mind. Second, to take charge of your thinking, keeping good thoughts in and throwing bad ones out.

Chapter 3 NOTES

[1] Philippians 4:8

[2] Matthew 12:13

[3] Colossians 3:2

[4] Exodus 20:15; Ephesians 4:28

[5] John 8:44

[6] 1 Corinthians 14:33

[7] Hebrews 5:14

Chapter 4

Taking charge

I well remember my first day as Deputy Principal of a large school—my last job before moving into full-time Christian work. Wide-ranging responsibilities were now mine, and there was an anticipatory sparkle in my eye as I strode into the building, looking forward to tackling them.

'Just let me at 'em!' I murmured to myself, rubbing my hands in eager anticipation of the challenge.

That's how you should be feeling now. God himself has appointed you Deputy Principal of your mind. He himself remains in overall charge, but yours is the everyday responsibility for the smooth running of your thought-life.

'Right,' you respond in a businesslike tone. 'Now where's the best place to begin?'

Root issues

Begin by plugging the gaps that let in trouble.

Let's be practical about this. If your mind is in a mess, there is little point in trying to tidy it up internally while the gates stand wide open for more mess to keep coming in. Oil slicks at sea can be sprayed with detergent to disperse them and prevent serious pollution, but how much better to create and enforce laws that forbid oil tankers to flush out their tanks into the ocean. It pays to go to root issues.

I suggest, therefore, that you begin by checking out those entry points of your mind that we referred to in the last chapter. Put on your immigration officer's hat and let's take a tour of the border crossings where thoughts enter your mind.

Through the eye to the mind

First we come to *Eye Gate,* a broad entrance through which thousands of thoughts pour into your mind every day.

Check out here what you *read.* What newspapers and magazines do you regularly take? Is their material helpful and productive? Does it stimulate positive thoughts? Are the illustrations wholesome? If not, exercise your right to stop buying and reading these papers. What's the point in complaining, young man, that you are beset by sexual fantasies when you yourself let sexy pictures in through Eye Gate unchecked? Take charge here.

Girls, check out those romantic novels. They may seem harmless enough with their sweet scenes of love and togetherness where all is roses, moonlight, serenades and the sweet song of the nightingale—plus a generous dash of sex. The trouble is, they are largely unreal. You will never establish a sound relationship with any man if you are mentally comparing him with the 'too good to be true' characters in these stories of romance. Real men, I'm afraid, fall short of the perfection that exists only in the novelist's imagination. I'm not saying you should never read a romantic novel again. Just keep it in proportion and exercise control.

Serious literature

Nothing should escape your immigration checks, not even great literature.

Over the years I've had to deal with more than my fair share of depressed students, young people whose minds have almost cracked under the onslaught of the nihilistic philosophy in the required reading of some university or college course.

Modern literature seems to be the chief offender. I once had to sort out a twenty-year-old man, undoubtedly a Christian, who had taken an overdose after reading Camus and Sartre as part of his French course. Works which blatantly preach that life is absurd, a sick and pointless farce brought to a welcome conclusion by the ringing down of the curtain of death, cannot be read without some negative influence on your thought-life.

Some would argue that if we Christians are effectively to reach modern people with the gospel of Christ, we must understand what makes them tick. We must appreciate their disease before we can offer an appropriate cure. And that, they insist, means acquainting ourselves with the literature that governs their thinking.

Such an approach may be necessary in some cases. But for Christians to give themselves blanket permission to read what is sometimes moral garbage in literary disguise is asking for trouble.

You must be wise and scrupulously honest with yourself here. If you are of robust mind you may well be able to tackle some such projects without serious after-effects. But for many of God's people it would be to invite into their thought-life a Trojan horse. Be sensible. Don't pollute your mind for the sake of an academic qualification.

Screen stimuli

If reading matter is powerful in its thought-shaping potential, how much more so are television, the cinema and the internet. Their direct, graphic impact is enormous. The ready availability of videos, 'adult' TV channels and DVDs enables us, if we so wish, to watch a steady stream of violence, the occult, sex and perversion in the privacy of our own homes. As you stand at Eye Gate, answerable to God for what you allow in, be ruthless.

My wife and I once sat down to watch *The Deer Hunter*, the highly-acclaimed film about ordinary Americans sent to fight in Vietnam. The music we had heard before; it was delightful. We quickly found, however, that the film's vivid portrayal of murder, torture, blood and gore sickened us and, for the sake of our thought-life, we switched it off part way through.

'Yes, a typical out-of-this-world Christian response!' some would retort. 'The film is realistic. It portrays the horrors of war as they really are. You Christians are already too naïve in your cosy world of spirituality, without cushioning yourselves from reality even further by chickening out of watching such a film.'

Wrong! The world is indeed full of horror, and we want to see it put to rights. We want an end to war. But before we can put the *world* straight we must first learn to rule our individual *selves*—thought-life included. It is in the context of the renewing of the mind that Paul urges us: 'Do not be overcome by evil'.[1] Evil must be expelled from our thinking before it can be driven out of society.

Of course, if ever we find ourselves in a war situation, or any situation where we have to face torture or violence first-hand, we can count on God's grace being available to strengthen us and help us through. But he supplies his grace only for real situations, not for hypothetical or vicarious ones. If you ever have to face being tortured yourself, his grace will be there, but watching a film of someone else being tortured doesn't qualify.

Realism—a deception

Don't be lured into danger by the 'realism' argument. I refuse to fill my mind with the gross evils of the world, no matter how 'true to life' they may be, if by so doing I wound my own mental integrity and thus paralyse my ability to improve things. Only when my mind is filled with the positive values of God's kingdom can I wield any kingdom influence on society at large.

Some people can watch the atrocities in *The Deer Hunter* without turning a hair. To them it is kid's stuff, hardened as they are by regular viewing of far more appalling material. That's dangerous. They now need something even more horrific to stimulate their imagination and excitement, and so the film producers dig deeper into the pit to find it. What by God's book is evil these folk consider only mildly questionable or even normal. For them to call something evil it has to be truly horrendous.

God wants you to become, not less, but *more* sensitive in your moral judgments as you guard Eye Gate. As we noted earlier, in his view, the 'mature' are those who are able to distinguish good from evil to a greater degree than average.[2] Don't desensitise your mind by viewing the worst the world can offer.

As for TV, the internet, DVDs and the cinema, then,

watch what you watch! 'I made a covenant [agreement] with my eyes,' declared Job, 'not to look lustfully at a girl'.³ In other words, he laid down some ground rules about what was permitted into his mind through Eye Gate.

I encourage you to do the same.

Hear no evil

Ear Gate isn't as broad as Eye Gate but it is broad enough. Check out what you listen to.

Let's start with everyday conversation. The language of the world is the language of complaint, pessimism and criticism. Our own citizenship, by contrast, is in heaven, where the native tongue is thanksgiving and praise. That makes us 'foreigners' in secular society. But we are more than tourists; we are active imperialists, set on turning the world into heaven's colony. 'Your kingdom come on earth, as it is in heaven,' we cry to the King who sent us on our mission of conquest.

Why is it, then, that instead of maintaining and propagating our natural language of thanksgiving and praise we allow the language of the majority to mould *us?*

'Oh dear, I see the price of petrol has gone up yet again,' we say as we chat in the supermarket. 'And hasn't the weather been terrible for the last few days? It's all these greenhouse gases, you know. Makes you wonder what the world's coming to, doesn't it?'

Don't allow your daily mingling with people who talk this way to get inside you and drag down your own attitude of mind. Gossip, criticism, belly-aching and moaning don't suit God's people. Set a guard at Ear Gate. Let the locals at the border post shout their negatives as much as they like, but don't let them over the line into your mind. If they get through, they will soon have you speaking the same language as themselves. Perish the thought!

The power of music

Then there's the music traffic to watch out for. It can be helpful, calming, emotionally uplifting. It can also be soul-destroying. Don't complain that your mind is being blown apart if you make no attempt to deny entry to saboteurs with musical time-bombs.

It is no sweeping statement, in my considered opinion, to say that much of the 'music' produced in the western pop music industry is a harmful influence on the mind.

All music consists of three elements: *melody* (the tune you can hum or whistle), *harmony* (sounds in combination) and *rhythm* (the beat). The best music, I believe, combines all three elements in balance. Melody is what gives a song its lasting (some would say 'spiritual') quality. One of my favourite songs from the melodic point of view—I'm not so keen on the words—and one I would love to have written myself, is the Lennon-McCartney song *Yesterday*. Beautiful!

Harmony is soulish, emotional. Certain chord combinations bring spontaneous tears to my eyes, especially when played by a brass band! And harmonies on a Hammond organ produce gut-level spasms of delight. Rhythm is the physical element that gets our hands clapping, body swaying and feet tapping.

Out of balance

Much modern music lacks balance between the elements. It is virtually devoid of melody, sparse in harmony and big on rhythm. Its insistent beat can have a numbing, hypnotic effect, opening up the mind to the suggestions of the words, which as often as not are of questionable content. This kind of music can become addictive. I have known people hooked on it the same way they get hooked on heroin. Rob them of a constant supply and they go to pieces.

Music—all music—somehow has the ability to influence the mind and emotions directly, without passing through the normal channels of logical analysis. Its influence can be for profit or for loss. Take care, then, what you listen to.

'I just can't break free of depression,' confessed a young man of twenty-two. 'And I keep getting strong impulses to do things that are violent, destructive and sexually perverted.'

My questioning revealed that he was a devotee of 'heavy metal' music. Every spare moment saw him sitting with the headphones on, blasting his brain with this rubbishy stuff. No wonder he felt a monster rising up within him. While his music wasn't the only factor in the equation, it was a major one. He found deliverance, but prevention is always better than cure.

Judge music with your spirit. Is it wholesome, uplifting, beautiful, edifying? If not, even though it be composed or performed by the world's most famous musician, turn it off. You're in charge, remember!

Chapter 4 NOTES

[1] Romans 12:2, 21

[2] Hebrews 5:14

[3] Job 31:1

Chapter 5

Taming the memory

No, this isn't a course on how to develop a photographic memory and so succeed in your studies without even trying.

Memory is important, however, because it provides another major gateway by which harmful thoughts can enter your mind. You may effectively control what enters by Eye Gate and Ear Gate but, if you fail to establish equal checks at *Memory Gate,* a whole host of troublesome guerrilla-thoughts will keep invading the mental territory over which God has put you in command.

Hamstrung Christians

Thousands of Christians today are hamstrung in their longings to serve the Lord as a result of leaving this entry point unguarded. Here are some typical cases.

John is in a housegroup meeting when he feels a prophetic word forming in his spirit. He is just about to deliver it when his mind speaks up: 'What a nerve! Who do you think you are? You once fiddled the office accounts. Oh yes, I know it was only once, and in a small way at that, and I know it all came out and that you got away with a severe reprimand. Yes, I know you repented. But *what's done can never be undone.* You've no right to prophesy in the meeting, you sinful wretch.'

So John keeps quiet. The people miss out on a word from

the Lord. John becomes pensive and sad. The devil jumps with glee.

Sexual abuse

Angela started going out with Bill six months ago. Everyone thinks it's an ideal partnership and has been giving them lots of encouragement. But Angela is beginning to panic. She really loves Bill and in many ways marriage is an exciting prospect, but her mind is in turmoil.

'Remember what Uncle Andy used to do to you,' says her mind, referring to the sexual interference Angela suffered as a child. 'You're soiled, second-hand goods now, far too cheap and dirty to make a good wife for a fine young man like Bill. And besides, you know full well that the whole sexual side of life is disgusting. If you really love this guy, the best thing you can do for him is to get out of his life.'

She breaks off the relationship. Bill is heartbroken and Angela, who already hated herself because of her past, despises herself even more now for having caused such hurt to the man she truly loves. She has had two boyfriends before, and both relationships came to a similar end. A clear pattern is now established: she is convinced she will never marry.

Bitterness

Stuart, an accountant, has been approached by the elders about becoming a deacon in the church. They have come to know of his ability in the financial realm and would like him to help in the treasury. He is thrilled at the privilege offered to him, but immediately feels guilty.

'How can you accept this offer when you're still so full of

bitterness over what George did to you?' argues his mind.

He had never been close to George, a fellow-Christian, but their relationship had plummeted to an all-time low at a church social gathering. George had cast a quick glance in his direction and commented, 'I've yet to find an accountant who's a man of faith.'

The people standing around all laughed. So did Stuart, but he wasn't laughing inside. George's comment had pierced like cold steel. He had always considered himself a man of faith. It was a wicked and hurtful thing for George to say! Things festered in his mind for some time before he realised that, in the light of Matthew 18:15-17, it was up to him to confront George and tackle the issue head on. He did so. George seemed genuinely sorry and asked for forgiveness, which Stuart freely gave, so things were now technically sorted out.

I say 'technically' because here is the root of Stuart's current problem. Every time he sees Bill, all the old feelings of hurt and bitterness well up. 'It's obvious,' he reasons to himself, 'that though I *thought* I'd forgiven him I haven't really done so at all. I'm not fit to serve as a deacon as long as I'm like this.'

So Stuart declines the elders' offer. The church treasury loses out on his abilities. And, worst of all, Stuart settles into the conviction that he will never be fit for anything because the bitterness is likely to last all his life.

House arrest

Now you can see how vital it is to guard Memory Gate. If this entrance is one favoured, as it is, by thoughts intent on paralysing your spiritual growth and practical success, you must be especially vigilant here.

The problem is that, whereas you can guard the other gates by stopping undesirable thoughts from entering your mind in the first place, with Memory Gate you are dealing with thoughts that claim to belong. After all, we are talking about past experiences, events that actually happened. And since they happened in your own life they are in a real sense part of *you*. They are inside already. What, then, should you do?

Put them under house arrest.

Memory Gate is the door to that section of your mind where you keep those bitter thoughts from the past under lock and key. You post a guard, not to prevent them getting into your active mind from outside, but to stop them getting into it from the *inside*. I am not talking about suppression. That is not the Christian way. I am talking about facing up to the events behind these troublesome thoughts, dealing with them positively and practically in accordance with Scripture, then refusing to have the issues raised ever again.

Forgive and forget

There is a lot of truth in the old adage, 'Forgive and forget'. It may not be a biblical expression but it is certainly a biblical sentiment.[1]

Forgiving comes first. John's major need is to forgive himself for fiddling the office accounts. *God* has forgiven him,[2] so why should John be tougher on himself than God?

Angela needs to forgive Uncle Andy, even though it was indeed a gross sin that he committed against her. It might have happened in the dim and distant past—and Uncle Andy may have been dead for years—but she still needs to forgive him from her heart.

Stuart has already followed proper biblical procedures in confronting George over his hurtful remark and has openly forgiven him.

So why are all three still in mental bondage? Because they have overlooked the second part of the formula: Forgive *and forget.*

Power to forget

'Do you mean we can forget just like that?' you may well ask, with a note of scepticism. 'It was radical enough being told I was responsible for my thinking generally, but surely you aren't suggesting, are you, that I have the power and responsibility to forget?'

Yes. But we need to be clear what is meant by 'forget' in this context. Consider for a moment how God forgets. What does he mean, for example, when he declares, 'I will forgive their wickedness and will *remember* their sins *no more'?*[3] Does he have a special memory-destruct facility? Hardly, because that would make him less than the omniscient (all-knowing) God that Scripture declares him to be.

No. When, having first forgiven, God goes on to 'forget', he is saying in effect: 'The issue is now resolved; the file is closed; the matter is buried once for all. I hereby determine that *I will never bring it up again.'* So don't keep coming back to God and reminding him about your old sins, once they have been forgiven. He will simply say, 'Not interested.'

We are called to adopt the same attitude. We certainly don't have the power to forget in the sense of 'deleting the file' from the computer at the touch of some mental button, but we can certainly forget in the same way that God does, *by refusing to let the issue be raised in our thinking again.*

No pity!

John, Angela and Stuart keep hearing their bad old memories wailing through the prison-house window, 'Let me out!' They take pity on them, turn them loose and soon find that the rascals have taken over.

Understand this: there is no room for pity towards these painful memories. They are guerrillas trained by Satan to wear you down and ruin all your joy in Christ, your inner peace, your sense of purpose and your usefulness to the Lord. So keep them under house arrest. Close your ears to their pleas to be let out. Don't entertain them at all. Turn your back on them, rattle the jail keys to show who's in charge, and get on with living in the beautiful light of God's forgiveness.

After a while these memories will begin to realise that you are no longer a soft touch and will keep relatively quiet, though you can expect them to try it on from time to time, all through your life. Don't *ever* take pity on them. Incorrigible villains that they are, they should never be offered remission for what looks like good behaviour. Determine here and now that they are going to stay put away for a life sentence, that is, for the duration of *your* natural life.

Getting them locked away in the first place can sometimes be a struggle, but as you arm yourself with the sword of the Word and the shield of faith you can be confident of success. In one or two rare cases you may need help from your fellow-Christians, but that will be the subject of a later chapter.

A fifth column?

There is one more gateway to your mind that we must mention: *Habit Gate*.

Some Christians believe that they are rotten through and through. After all, didn't Jesus say, *'From within,* out of men's hearts, come *evil thoughts,* sexual immorality, theft, murder, adultery, greed, malice, deceit, lewdness, envy, slander, arrogance and folly. All these evils come *from inside...'*?[4]

'What's the point,' they argue, 'of manning our defences against the intrusion of evil thoughts from outside, or of keeping bad memories locked up in our internal "forgettery", if there is a fifth column inside—something sinful within our very nature guaranteeing a regular supply of undesirable thoughts to trouble our minds? We might as well throw in the towel right away and resign ourselves to mental turmoil for the rest of our days.'

How typical of the devil to get us thinking the worst when God has given us every cause to think the best! The words of Jesus about evil thoughts coming from inside may be true of the unregenerate, as both Scripture and experience amply confirm. But if you are a genuine born-again child of God this is not, repeat *not* true of you.

What sort of salvation would it be if God simply wiped the slate clean and then left us to muddle on, with our basic nature unchanged? As it is, he has dealt with the issue at root level. 'If anyone is in Christ, he is *a new creation; the old has gone, the new has come!*[5]

The old bias

Your old nature certainly had a bias towards evil. Like the lead weight inside a 'wood' in the game of bowls, it used to pull you off course, away from God's 'strait and narrow'. Not that you *wanted* to stay on God's course most of the time. The struggle probably began when you started to feel your way towards him—the awful struggle of trying to live up to God's standards by will power and self-effort. What a killer!

Paul describes that conflict in Romans chapter 7. As a devout Jew trying hard to keep the law of God he found himself up against impossible odds, because his inner nature wasn't yet changed: 'What I do is not the good I want to do; no, the evil I do not want to do—this I keep on doing' (v19). Paul didn't have this struggle all his life, however, as Romans chapter 8 makes clear, and neither should you. An essential part of the gospel is the inner renewal that takes place. The evil bias is replaced by a godly one.

Programmed to please God

As Christians we now 'participate in the *divine* nature'.[6] We have had a completely new start, a radical refit from the inside out, having been 'born again, not of perishable seed, but of imperishable'.[7] That seed remains within us[8] as *a new bias, constantly pushing us in the direction of godliness.*

This is the glory of the new covenant. No longer is God's will something outside us, permanently beyond our grasp because of a sinful nature. On the contrary, God promised, 'I will put my laws *in their hearts,* and I will write them *on their minds'.*[9] To use computer terminology, we're now programmed to please God.

Creatures of habit

What, then, about the ungodly impulses that we sometimes feel? Where do they come from? What is the source of the evil thoughts that trouble us from time to time—assuming that we have blocked their entry point at Eye Gate and Ear Gate and have kept Memory Gate securely locked?

They come through Habit Gate. We are creatures of habit because God made us that way. I remember changing my car once and finding for a week or two that, whenever I signalled a turn, the windscreen wipers came on. The controls were on opposite sides from their position in the old car and, being a creature of habit, it took me some time to get into the new way.

If that is true in such minor areas of life, how much more is it true of the major ones like character development and the mastery of the mind. Up until the time you were born again your life was marked by ungodly patterns of behaviour. Sinful thinking was the norm. Now that you have come to Christ your essential nature has been changed into a godly one, but that does not make you perfect overnight, as you well know. No, because you are a creature of habit it will take time and effort on your part to renew your mind and behaviour, to bring them *in practice* into line with what you are *in principle* in Christ.

No entry

Recognise, then, that many of the unwelcome thoughts you discover in your mind have crept in through Habit Gate. Put a guard there, too.

Challenge each one that tries to get in. It won't take kindly to your challenge but will cry out in indignation, 'What are you talking about? I've been coming in and out of here un-challenged for years!'

Don't take any notice. Simply insist, 'Get out! I know you used to wander in and out as you liked, but there has been a change of management here and you're now a prohibited immigrant.' Then boot it out of your mind, snatching its passport away as you do so.

Cover all the entry points to your mind this way. Let a vigilant guard be posted at Eye Gate, Ear Gate, Memory Gate and Habit Gate—all of them. Let the devil see that when God hands out mind-monitoring responsibilities, you take them seriously.

Chapter 5 NOTES

[1] Jeremiah 31:34; Hebrews 10:17; Isaiah 43:25; etc.

[2] 1 John 1:9

[3] Jeremiah 31:34

[4] Mark 7:21-23

[5] 2 Corinthians 5:17

[6] 2 Peter 1:4

[7] 1 Peter 1:23

[8] 1 John 3:9

[9] Hebrews 10:16

Chapter 6

Pulling down strongholds

Brian's garden had always been the finest in the street. He took great delight in hedge-trimming, weeding, pruning, hoeing, composting, planting and mowing the lawn. In fact, every spare minute saw him out of the house and in the garden, keeping it in tip-top order.

He had tackled some major projects in his time: lopping a massive sycamore that kept out valuable light; constructing a pond, with waterfall and fountain; building his own greenhouse; and laying a completely new lawn.

But today Brian was beaten.

He and Ruth had a growing family and for some time the need for more space had pointed to a move. Today that move had taken place. Though their new home was only a mile away, it seemed like a different world. It wasn't just the extra space or the fact that they were on a different bus route; it was the garden.

'Garden' was in fact a euphemism; 'jungle' would be a better word. Clearly it hadn't been touched for years. The grass was a metre tall. All the shrubs had gone wild. Overgrown roses mingled with every weed imaginable, with nettles dominant. What a mess! For the first time in his gardening life, Brian conceded defeat. He could keep on top of any garden once it was in some sort of basic order, but the state this one was in, it would take every spare moment for the next five years to make any kind of impression on it. What was he to do?

The answer was obvious: *call on his friends for help.*

'Many hands...'

Brian sent out an invitation to a dozen of the most fit and muscular among them. 'Come along to our garden party next Saturday,' it read, adding, 'Bring your own spade.' On the day, they all turned up at 8.30am prompt and set to work. Except Gareth, who didn't arrive till nine; he'd been to the tool hire place to get a rotavator for the day.

By seven in the evening a total transformation had taken place. It didn't exactly look like Kew Gardens, but the whole area was dug over, the bushes were trimmed back, all the dead plants were pulled out and the stones (and a rusty old bike frame) removed. From here on, Brian could comfortably tackle the garden on his own.

Some Christians have minds like the garden at Brian's new house. If their mental conflicts were only minor ones, they could no doubt keep on top by dealing with intrusive thoughts in the way we have described. But when the mind is in a real mess, they take one look and say, 'There's no way I can handle this on my own.'

Military strongholds

Paul uses a different illustration—a military one—when he talks about 'strongholds' of the mind.[1]

The forces of the enemy (alien thoughts) can, for the most part, be driven out of our mental territory bit by bit as we exert our spiritual authority and use the weapons of prayer and holy determination. But some of them retreat to a stronghold and barricade themselves in. They smile confidently at the stout walls and massive doors that they have built into the fortification for just such an eventuality. Then, from the top of the tower, they peer down and laugh at our feeble efforts to get them out.

Do you remember Angela, whom we met in the last chapter? She knew her Bible and understood her rights doctrinally, but somehow she seemed unable to move into an appropriation of them. She felt powerless before the stronghold in her mind. The enemy shouted from the turret, 'You'll never marry. Not for you a satisfying relationship with any man, and we're here to see that nothing changes in that respect. You're ruined for life!'

Such thoughts have no business occupying mental territory that Jesus has bought for himself at the price of his own blood. But they claim squatters' rights and refuse to budge.

Right of usage

Not far from my home, a long-established footpath winds its way across some fields, joining two housing areas. Some time ago, the farmer who owned the land decided to fence it off and raise crops on it. Suddenly, walkers along the path found their way barred by a wood and barbed-wire fence.

There was a long legal battle. The farmer claimed that he owned the land and was entitled to do what he liked with it. But in the end he had to give in and re-open the path simply because it had been used by so many people for so many years. The law gave the walkers 'right of way by virtue of usage'.

This is the approach that is always taken by the thoughts

and attitudes that occupy mental strongholds. 'We've been around here for years,' they remind us. 'This mind of yours is home to us now. It may be true that you've been bought out by Jesus and are now under his management, but we claim the right of usage—we're not moving!'

But this legal battle is fought by a different book. There is no clause in King Jesus' Charter giving users' rights to agents of the enemy. They can argue their case as long and as hard as they like, but because Jesus claims sovereign rights, with no exceptions at all, they eventually have to give in and go. Their stronghold *has* to crumble.

A joint offensive

You may have such strongholds in your own mind. From the tower top they fly a different flag from that of King Jesus, whose rule they arrogantly refuse to acknowledge. These strongholds are areas of thinking where you seem unable to take control, areas that appear to have a will of their own. Perhaps you have battled for years to win the victory, but without success because these intrusive thoughts, like the grass and weeds in Brian's garden, have a 'strong hold' on your mind.

If that is the case, it is time to call in your friends for the military equivalent of Brian's 'garden party.' It is time for a joint offensive against the occupying forces, one that will blast their stronghold to smithereens and send them scurrying for the border.

For some people, the idea of calling for outside help can be a terrifying prospect. To do so is to expose one's weakness, and nobody enjoys doing that. It becomes doubly difficult in the traditional religious context that has become normal for so many. Church life that consists merely of attending services and looking at the back of someone's neck for an hour provides no basis for the kind of spiritual co-operation needed to pull down strongholds of the mind.

Strength in relationship

Happily, things are changing. More and more Christians are discovering that church, in the real sense of the word, means living relationships.

The ancient Preacher understood this vital principle. He observed that, 'Two are better than one... If one falls down, his friend can help him up. But pity the man who falls and has no-one to help him up!'[2] Certainly this is a truth that the Holy Spirit is highlighting in our generation. In fact, I strongly suspect that the Lord allows certain situations to develop beyond our individual control for the express purpose of pointing us towards honest, open relationships where mutual help can be given and received.

Do you have someone to help you? Someone to stand alongside you and join his or her strength to yours for the pulling down of a mental stronghold? I sincerely hope so. If not, find someone. Ask the Lord to direct you to some capable Christian to whom you can open your heart, express your need and put in a request for help. Don't worry that your admission of need might cause such a person to look down on you or withdraw from you. All Christians have needs of one kind or another. Far from alienating friendship, your admission of need is far more likely to cement it. Genuine believers in Christ count it, not a burden, but a joy and privilege to help one another.

Do not, however, approach anyone who is loose-tongued

or inexperienced. You may choose to go to one of your church leaders, who will doubtless have counselled and helped others in similar situations. In fact, if he is a true pastor, the chances are that he will be aware of your need already and will have been praying that you would ask for help rather than wait for him to raise the matter with you.

It may well be that more than one person will join with you in specific prayer. There are often distinct advantages in that. If you are a woman, the presence of another woman will help you feel more relaxed.

Lessons in demolition

The first step is to pinpoint the root issue. There is no point in bringing in the heavy artillery if you don't know the stronghold's location.

No doubt you will converse for a while. You will explain the need as you perceive it—the way negative thoughts seem to dominate you, your inability to break free, and so on. Your counsellor, out of his experience, will no doubt ask questions calculated to clarify understanding, perhaps explaining to you some aspects that had escaped your notice.

He may also have insights or information about your situation given supernaturally to ensure that the stronghold is finally destroyed. Don't be surprised or alarmed at this. It is just one of the weapons with 'divine power to demolish strongholds' that the Lord has provided.

Once the stronghold has been precisely located it may be helpful to be reminded of your rights in Christ, such as the right to a sound mind,[3] the right to live victoriously[4] and the right to be on top of your circumstances.[5] A wise pastor will also encourage you by outlining (without naming names) cases he has known where Christians with similar problems to yours have found release.

The word of authority

Then he will pray for you, calling upon the Lord to meet your specific need. He may also speak directly to the stronghold in your mind, addressing it authoritatively in the name of Jesus and commanding it to yield to the King upon whose territory it has been so presumptuously built.[6] In Angela's case, for example, he might declare, 'In Jesus' name I break the hold of the enemy that has locked up this girl into the fear of a lasting relationship with a man. I command you, prison of past experience, to yield up the mind and emotions that have been held captive within you. Here and now I break your bondage!'

Your own faith will rise in response, and you may well want to join in the pounding of the stronghold by praying yourself, telling the entrenched thoughts that you are not putting up with them any longer and ordering them out.

Your counsellor may then speak into your life the positive values that have hitherto been kept out. Having demolished the stronghold, he is now building on the same site a living memorial of faith, hope and love to the praise of the all-conquering Lord Jesus. To Angela he might say, 'I release you in the name of Jesus. I speak into existence in your mind and heart the ability to think normally, to feel normally and to relate normally. I declare to you that, in the Lord's eyes, you are a chaste virgin.'

Tackled this way, fortresses of the mind crumble and fall. Christ *must* conquer!

'Thank you, Lord!'

Thanksgiving is never out of place for the Christian,[7] so speak out your thanks to God at this stage. Say, 'Thank you, Lord, for the victory that has been won in my life today. I'm free now! Thank you for the Christian friends who've stood alongside me in the battle. Thank you that I'm never going to be the same again, Lord, because the stronghold *has* been demolished and you now rule supreme in my mind and in my whole being.'

Now remember Brian the gardener. Once his friends had been in to help him clear the jungle, he could maintain the garden himself, not only keeping it clear of weeds but actually improving it. It is the same with you: once the groundwork has been done with the help of others, you can keep your thought life in good order and improve its quality *on your own*.

But more about that in the next chapter.

Chapter 6 NOTES

[1] 2 Corinthians 10:4-5

[2] Ecclesiastes 4:9-10

[3] 2 Timothy 1:7

[4] Romans 6:14

[5] Philippians 4:13

[6] See Matthew 17:20

[7] 1 Thessalonians 5:18

Chapter 7

Maintaining the victory

When Brian's friends shouted goodbye at the garden gate and made their way home after their hard day's work, it was the end of the job for them. But for Brian it was only the beginning. They had done the groundwork so that he could take over where they had left off.

There is a spiritual principle here, and failure to grasp it can plunge you into despair. I refer to the need to *hold on to and build upon what you have gained.* Far too often we hear statements like:

'The Lord healed me of eczema five years ago, but recently it has come back again.'

'When I was baptised in the Holy Spirit I gave up smoking just like that, after being a smoker for twenty years. It was amazing. But I was under pressure at work recently and started smoking again.'

'I broke out of my shyness problem quite dramatically when they prayed for me at a conference, but it didn't last. I'm as shy now as I ever was, I'm afraid.'

Such statements make me very sad. They also cause a holy indignation to rise up within me, because such lapses need not happen. And, besides, I hate giving the enemy cause for rejoicing.

Faith that acts

Why, then, do such lapses take place?

First and foremost because many of God's people have fallen for *the lie that we have to remain passive*. 'Just relax and give Almighty God room to act,' they say. 'Let go and let God. You don't have to *do* anything; in fact you *can't* do anything. So stop trying.'

What do you think of that? You probably feel a bit confused. 'Maybe there's some truth in it,' you venture. 'After all, doesn't the Bible say that the righteous will live by faith?[1] And what about that verse that says, "You will not have to fight this battle. Take up your positions; stand firm and see the deliverance the Lord will give you"?[2] And on another occasion didn't David say, "The battle is the Lord's"?'[3]

Well, let's examine those statements. Certainly the righteous will live by faith. But as James is at pains to remind us in his letter, faith is never passive; *faith acts.*

What is more, the people who were commanded to 'stand firm' remained far from passive. Read the story for yourself. Yes, the Lord supernaturally dealt with their enemies, but they themselves acted in the light of that. In fact, their 'standing firm' involved five things: they believed the promise; they praised and worshipped the Lord; they marched out to face the enemy; they gave thanks to God; and they spent three days collecting the plunder.

As for David, after declaring, 'The battle is the Lord's', he promptly went out against Goliath with his sling and stones. You can hardly call that being passive!

A personal Jericho

There is a difference between trying to do God's work *for* him and doing God's work *with* him. The one will drive you to despair; the other will lead you to victory. You must act, but it must be in faith.

You may find it helpful to look upon the demolishing of a mental stronghold as a personal Jericho. Jericho, you will recall, was the great city that the Israelites faced when they first crossed the River Jordan into the Promised Land. They marched around it for seven days, at God's command. Then, at the blowing of the trumpets, the city walls collapsed, allowing the Israelites to pour in and make the victory complete. God did the basic work; they cashed in on it, so to speak.

Let's suppose that you have had a personal Jericho. You and your friends have claimed the promises of God and seen the walls of some mental stronghold come tumbling down. What a triumph! But now what?

You must move on from there to 'take captive every thought to make it obedient to Christ'. Just as Joshua believed *and acted upon* God's 'I will give you every place where you set your foot',[4] you must go out and actively set foot on every square centimetre of your mental territory. Patrol it, guard it, exploit it, develop it. Rule it for Christ.

A brazen 'Good morning!'

Keep a particularly watchful eye on Habit Gate. Worry, smoking, shyness and a host of old-style thoughts will march back through with a brazen 'Good morning!' and a cheery smile—unless you keep guard. Once inside, the smile will disappear and they will start rebuilding the old fortress with walls stouter than ever. The chances are that the odd one will succeed in getting through. Don't worry. Don't sigh and say, 'Oh well, it was worth a try, and it was nice while it lasted, but I suppose permanent mental victory is really too much to expect.' Never settle for defeat. As soon as you spot an intruder, bellow at him like a sergeant-major, 'Hey, you there! Get out of here and stay out!' To reinforce your point, grab it by the scruff of the neck and throw it over the border of your mind, with a boot up the backside to help it on its way.

That's how faith works—nothing namby-pamby, just decisive, robust action.

Demolition—it's a fact

All this, of course, is of little avail if you don't really believe that the stronghold has been demolished in the first place.

Imagine a hard-up fellow called Fred who lives below the poverty line. He has a bank account but hasn't written a cheque for months because his balance stands at only £2.50. Then he receives a letter from a solicitor informing him that he has been left £500,000 in his Great Uncle Albert's will, the said sum having now been credited to his account.

'It's too good to be true,' says Fred to himself. 'Besides, I didn't even know I had a Great Uncle Albert. It must be a hoax.'

So he continues living in poverty. He stays poor because he *thinks* he's poor, while in fact he is rich. He stays clothed in rags and continues to eat stale crusts when he could be writing cheques at clothes stores and restaurants.

The point is, if you *believe* you are poor, you might as well be, even though you are in fact rich. Or, if you believe the mental stronghold is still standing, it might as well be, even though it is in fact demolished.

What will alter Fred's approach? He should get out the solicitor's letter and read it right through several times, letting its message sink in. He should check the name and address on the letterhead against the phone book or, better still, visit the address personally to verify its existence. He should ask the bank for an up-to-date statement of his account and feast his eyes on all those zeroes in the figure £500,002.50!

Best of all, he should start writing cheques and rejoice when they don't bounce. He *is* rich!

And what should the doubting Christian do? Like Fred, he should study the documentary evidence—in this case what Scripture has to say about victory in Christ. He should read and reread, for instance, the words of Jesus in Matthew 18:19: 'If two of you on earth agree about anything you ask for, it will be done for you by my Father in heaven.' He should have a word with the 'bank manager'—the Holy Spirit—whose pleasure it is to assure us of the benefits we have in Christ.

Best of all, he should start 'writing cheques'. That is, he should start taking active steps that take for granted the demolition of the mental stronghold, and rejoice when he makes progress. He *is* victorious!

The homosexual

Let's look at a couple of examples of how this works, one contemporary and one biblical.

Richard was in his late twenties when I first got to know him, a quiet and thoughtful Christian with a delightful sense of humour. I sensed that he had difficulties relating to women but waited to see if he would raise the issue.

As our friendship developed, he found enough confidence to open his heart to me. He was homosexually oriented, he said. He found himself physically attracted to men rather than to women. Though he longed to marry and have a family in the normal way, and had attempted to develop a friendship with several girls, he had opted out of each friendship as things became serious, fearing that he would not be able to consummate a physical relationship because of his homosexual leanings.

My questions revealed that his mother had been dominant to the point of 'smothering' him (his own word). She had, in fact, wanted a girl and for a long time had dressed Richard in girls' clothes. To make matters worse, Richard had been interfered with sexually in his early teens by a male relative. No wonder his mind was in confusion.

First we cleared the ground: God creates no-one homosexual. Scripture is abundantly clear that God-given sexuality is heterosexual and that heterosexual relationships within marriage are the only ones that enjoy the blessing of God.

Richard accepted that. 'I know it's true, and I desperately want to be normal,' he assured me.

Perversion's impertinence

Next, I pointed out that Satan had a stronghold in his mind. Richard's knowing the truth doctrinally and academically was one thing; acting on it was something altogether different. Every time he tried to think and act normally he faced a barrage of arrows, rocks and boiling oil from the alien thoughts occupying the battlements of his mental fortress.

'We've decided you're homosexual,' they shouted, 'and don't you dare try to shift us!'

What a nerve!

A colleague and I prayed with Richard. All the time and effort were in the discussion beforehand; the actual praying didn't take more than ten minutes. We declared the victory of Jesus. We addressed the alien thoughts in the mental stronghold and commanded their surrender. We demolished the fortress in the name of Jesus. We made a prophetic declaration of Richard's freedom.

Richard himself joined in the praying, and we all finished up giving thanks that the work was done and that Richard was now both free and normal.

Rearguard action

Some time later he met a young lady and a friendship developed which looked promising. She was a sweet girl, and we all hoped the relationship would develop into something permanent. For a while, all went well. Then one day Richard confessed to me that the old thoughts about being homosexual and incapable of a normal relationship were crowding in on his mind again.

'Of course they are,' I told him. 'The alien thoughts don't take kindly to being kicked out of their stronghold and now they're trying to convince you that nothing has changed. Everything is going the way one would expect. Just remember, Richard, the stronghold *has* been demolished. Take a tough line with these lying thoughts. Throw them out, reminding yourself of who you are in Christ.'

Not long afterwards, Richard asked the girl to marry him.

The engagement took place and, later, a lovely wedding. Now, many years later, Richard is still a happy husband and father—all because he dared to believe that the stronghold was broken and acted in keeping with the prophetic word of release.

Timid Tim

Timothy's problem was a different one: he was just plain timid.[5] In spite of being a protégé of the great apostle Paul, one imagines him to have been a poor mixer, preferring, no doubt, to keep a low public profile. Certainly he was no good at confrontation,

But in other ways he was very gifted, and his knowledge of Scripture was second to none, thanks to the training given by his godly mother and grandmother.[6] Paul recognised his potential for leadership and took him in hand.

What exactly happened we don't know, but from the two letters sent to him by Paul we can piece together a broad picture. There was one occasion when Paul and the elders prayed specifically for Timothy, giving him personal prophecies for his encouragement and direction.[7] I suspect that part of the prophetic word was to do with Timothy's need to overcome his natural timidity.

It is easy to imagine the group of leaders standing round him, together demolishing the stronghold of timidity in his mind by concerted prayer.

I can hear Paul making a prophetic declaration: 'Timothy, in the Lord you're no longer timid; you're bold! Scripture declares the righteous to be as bold as a lion, and you are righteous in Christ. Be strong, therefore, to speak the truth without fear or favour and to confront error with boldness. Today I confer upon you the very boldness of God himself.

Use it as a weapon in the cause of Christ.'

Living it out

Timothy began to live in the good of that experience, I'm sure. But, being human, he had doubts from time to time, especially when circumstances required confrontation. 'Can I really handle this?' He would ask himself. 'Or am I the same timid Tim that I was as a youngster?'

Years later, Timothy found himself in a situation needing confrontation in Ephesus, where he was keeping an eye on the local church for Paul. It had come to his attention that there was a group of odd-balls in the church, people who were causing no end of trouble by their eccentric teachings. Paul's instruction to Timothy concerning these people was painfully clear: he was to 'command' them 'not to teach false doctrines any longer'.[8]

'Command' is a tough word. How much easier it would have been if Paul had said, 'Have a quiet word in their ear and suggest that they cool it a bit.' But when the truth of God is at stake, action must be bold—and the once-timid Timothy was the man chosen to issue the command.

'In keeping with...'

Paul knew how hard this would be for him, but he didn't back down. Instead, he reminded Timothy of the prophetic word given so long before and encouraged him to act in line with it.

'Timothy, my son,' he wrote, 'I give you this instruction [that is, the instruction to command silence upon the false teachers] *in keeping with the prophecies once made about you, so that by following them you may fight the good fight*'.[9]

Do you see the principle now? The demolition of his mental stronghold didn't turn Timothy into a fearless confronter overnight, so that he could silence false teachers without even trying. No, he had to keep on acting 'in keeping with' what had taken place on that crucial day.

You are in the same boat as both Richard and Timothy. You will need to maintain the victory in exactly the same way, and to do it for the rest of your life. The power of the Holy Spirit that indwelt them is at your disposal, too. They maintained the mental victory. There is no reason why you should not do the same.

In the battle for the mind you *can* be conqueror. So break free. Then live free, maintaining your victory by active faith. Enjoy the privilege that is yours as part of your birthright in Christ: a sound mind.

Chapter 7 NOTES

[1] Romans 1:17, quoting Habakkuk 2:4

[2] 2 Chronicles 20:17

[3] 1 Samuel 17:47

[4] Joshua 1:3

[5] 1 Corinthians 16:10; 2 Timothy 1:4,7-8

[6] 2 Timothy 1:5; 3:15

[7] 1 Timothy 1:18; 4:14; 2 Timothy 1:6

[8] 1 Timothy 1:3

[9] 1 Timothy 1:18

Chapter 8

Food for thought

Nature, we are told, abhors a vacuum. No sooner does a vacuum appear (as when lightning flashes) than something rushes in to fill it (a violent in-surge of air, producing a clap of thunder). The same principle operates in the realm of the mind. A mind emptied of thoughts becomes a mental vacuum; thoughts will come rushing in to fill it.

But what kind of thoughts? The devil, of course, will always be quick to send in some of his own variety. You must be alert to his constant attempts, given half a chance, to push into your mind all sorts of mental garbage. For this very reason, avoid at all costs any kind of mental or spiritual 'therapy'—such as yoga, transcendental meditation or hypnosis—that counsels you to 'let your mind go blank'. To let it go blank is to invite the enemy to use it as a litter bin.

So far, in our search for a sound mind, we have concentrated on how to deal with unbidden thoughts: throw the bad ones out, entertain the good ones and then set up border checks at the gateways to the mind—Eye Gate, Ear Gate, Memory Gate and Habit Gate. In other words, we have focused on keeping out the rubbish.

But you must not stop there. As we have just seen, to empty the mind of rubbish, and then do no more, is to run the risk of creating a dangerous vacuum. Hand in hand with the emptying activity, therefore, goes the need to *fill your mind with positive and wholesome thoughts.*

Crowded out

I once read about a terrorist who planned to blow up a shopping complex. Having loaded a massive bomb into a stolen car, he drove to the complex on a busy Saturday afternoon, when the maximum number of people would be hurt in the explosion. The plan was to park the car, complete with time-bomb, in the roof-top car park of the shopping complex.

Unfortunately (or fortunately!), when he arrived, the 'Car Park Full' sign was displayed at the foot of the ramp and a policeman waved him on in the direction of the city outskirts. He couldn't get in to do his dirty work because the place was already full.

That is exactly what the mental time-bombers sent by Satan should find when they approach your mental territory: not a wide-open space with a sign saying 'Come right in and park where you like', but a mind so jam-packed with good, wholesome thoughts that they can't even get their noses inside.

The staple diet

So what kind of good material are we talking about? Well, what could be better and more wholesome than the Word of God? The Scriptures will always be the staple diet of a healthy mind.

'Oh dear, that rules me out, I'm afraid,' you may be saying. 'Bible study is OK for the brainy types, but I've never been a great reader and, if I'm honest, I find the Bible a very difficult book to understand.'

But I didn't suggest Bible *study*. Some people just don't have the kind of mind that slips easily into concentrated study. I once saw a book entitled *Everyone a Bible Student*. 'No chance,' I muttered to myself as I turned away.

What I *am* suggesting is that you *read* the Bible—a different thing altogether. Every literate Christian can do that. What is more, any book is more interesting when you know the author, and, assuming that you are a born-again believer, you are intimately acquainted with the Holy Spirit who inspired the Bible.[1]

Look upon the Scriptures as letters sent by the Lord specifically to you to express his love and his will to you. Could you ever yawn over love letters? Make sure you have a good, flowing translation such as the New International Version or the New Living Translation, and choose an edition with good-sized print so that you are able to read without straining your eyes. Or, if you have Bible software, you can read it on your computer screen. Then get into the habit of reading as often as you can.

Washing the wool

One way is to read big chunks at a time. Never mind if you come across bits you don't understand; just pass over and keep on reading. So, at one sitting, you might read right through one of the New Testament letters, or half of Mark's Gospel, or a dozen chapters of Isaiah, or a handful of Psalms.

'But the trouble is, I just don't seem to take much in. At the end I sometimes ask myself what I've just read, and as often as not I've little or no idea.'

Here we have a common complaint, to which I would reply, 'Never mind; just keep at it.'

'But what's the point of that?' you ask.

A Scottish lassie was once standing outside her Highland croft holding a round, tray-like object under a running tap. A passing tourist stopped to ask the way and, in so doing, saw that the object was a sieve containing wool.

'Poor girl,' he thought. 'She's obviously very simple-minded. Fancy trying to fill a sieve with water!'

When he pointed out to her that the water was going straight through the sieve, the girl gave him a withering look and retorted, 'Och aye, but it's washing the wool!'

You may feel that a sieve (not to mention the wool) is a perfect description of your mind as you read the Bible: nothing seems to stick in it. But be assured that the mere passage of the Word of God through your mind has a *cleansing* effect. In Africa I've seen something similar: freshly picked leafy vegetables being washed in a wicker basket wedged between rocks in the middle of a stream. The water doesn't stay in the basket; it flows straight through, washing the leaves in the process.

So keep at your Bible reading. Let it flow through you; more is being accomplished than you realise.

Browsing in the library

Don't feel that you must start at Genesis and press right through to Revelation. Jump around a bit. Some Christians feel dreadful twinges of conscience about this, remembering the frown and the wagging finger of their primary school teacher who pronounced, 'Not until you have read Book

Three of the reading scheme *right through* will I allow you to go on to Book Four.'

It may help you to remember that the Bible, while it is in one sense a single book, is also a library of sixty-six smaller books. Feel free to browse along the shelves, so to speak, and read the books in any order. God won't wag his finger at you!

As you read the Bible, ask yourself questions: What does this mean? How can I put that into practice? Why did the writer say that? Sometimes you may want to jot comments in the margin or in a notebook, or underline verses that particularly impress you. Get into the habit, too, of sharing with friends the insights you receive; it will both bless them and reinforce your own understanding.

The Bible—Mm!

Large volumes have been written on Bible reading, and I don't intend to write another. My particular concern is for your thought life, so I am going to highlight just two aspects of Bible reading that will be of help. They both begin with 'm'.

Often, when people are deep in thought, the only sound to escape their lips is 'Mm'. There you have it—double 'm' to link your thought life with the Word of God.

The first 'm' is *meditation*. 'I meditate on your precepts' said the Psalmist,[2] who points the way for you and me. Take one of those verses that has specially impressed you during your broad reading and let your mind dwell on it—that's what meditation means—a sentence at a time, a phrase at a time, or even a word at a time.

How to meditate

Take, for example, the first sentence of Psalm 23: 'The LORD is my shepherd.' You might begin by focusing on the last word: 'The LORD is my *shepherd.'* The eastern shepherd, upon whom this word-picture is based, really looks after his sheep, protecting them from predators, guiding them into good pastures, rescuing them when they fall down holes, calling them by name. Think how the Lord cares for you in similar ways.

Then let your attention settle on the first two words: *'The LORD* is my shepherd.' Wonderful! None other than the Lord of creation, the crucified, risen and glorified Christ Jesus, is directing your steps!

'The LORD *is* my shepherd.' Yes, there is no doubt about it. It is not just wishful thinking or a figment of the imagination. He really *is* your shepherd. You might not fully understand all the wonders of salvation (who does?), or be able to give logical answers to the agnostics, but by the inner witness of the Holy Spirit you just know, deep down inside, that the Lord *is* your shepherd.

'The Lord is *my* shepherd.' True, he looks after many other sheep as well, but, praise him, he cares personally for you!

Get the idea? To make Bible meditation of this kind a regular practice is to ensure a mind filled with wholesome thoughts. An alien thought trying to sneak in among such blessed company will be as obvious as a hippopotamus trying to sneak unnoticed into your bath.

Memorisation

The second 'm' is *memorisation*. 'Let the word of Christ dwell in you richly,' urges Paul.[3] Memorisation is an excellent way to do it. Yes, I know, you have the most appalling memory and sometimes can't even remember what day it is, so how can you be expected to commit Bible verses to memory?

By *disciplining* yourself to do it. '*Train* yourself to be godly', wrote Paul to Timothy, using an athletic term.[4] Any training involves time, effort and determination—and mental training is no exception. But the fruit it bears in terms of godliness and soundness of mind is well worth the effort. If you can remember the birthdays of your nephews and nieces or the order of the first six football clubs in the Second Division, you can memorise Scripture.

Don't set yourself an unrealistic target. If you have never done this kind of thing before, settle for memorising one Bible verse every two months—that is six per year. Should you find it easier than expected, you can always step up the pace later.

In time of need

One advantage in committing Scripture to memory is that it gives the Holy Spirit some material to work with when you find yourself in a difficult situation. To his disciples Jesus said, 'The Holy Spirit, whom the Father will send in my name, will...remind you of everything I have said to you'.[5]

Before the Holy Spirit could remind them, they had to hear Jesus speak. In the same way, you cannot expect the Holy Spirit to remind you of an appropriate Scripture truth in a time of need if that Scripture truth hasn't first been filed away in your memory. So take memorisation seriously.

Begin now. Soak your mind in the Scriptures until, like cloth soaked in dye, the two become inseparable and your thinking is permanently coloured by God's Word.

A 'thought-account'

Not that the only thoughts worth entertaining are Bible verses. Far from it. Recall Paul's advice that we referred to in an earlier chapter: 'Whatever is true, whatever is noble, whatever is right, whatever is pure, whatever is lovely, whatever is admirable—if anything is excellent or praiseworthy—*think about such things*.'[6]

Lots of things in life fit into those thought-worthy categories: people you love, beautiful places, heart-warming events, good jokes, acts of kindness and generosity, lovely music, swimming, hiking, standing on top of a mountain—the list is endless, and very personal. I keep a 'bank account' of precious thoughts. From time to time I will draw one out and let it fill my mind—especially when I can't sleep and my mind is full of restless thoughts. I calm the unsettled thoughts by gathering them all round one precious thought.

Sometimes it is a Bible verse, and, like the Psalmist, I meditate on the law of the Lord 'day *and night*'.[7] Or it may be a non-biblical thought. There's a beautiful spot in the Yorkshire Dales, for example, where my family and I have spent some memorable holidays. I can picture it now: the river burbling along over the rounded stones, with a little green footbridge leading to the far bank, which is lined with feathery larches. Two grey stone cottages huddle together nearby. On either side of the valley the great green hills rise up, criss-crossed with dry-stone walls and dotted with sheep, all under the blue canopy of a summer sky.

To take a mental stroll in that lovely landscape is to fill my mind with good and wholesome thinking, rejoicing in the goodness of God. I encourage you to build up your own 'bank account' of beautiful thoughts, your savings for a mental 'rainy day' of depression or siege.

Something beginning with 'G'

I couldn't close this chapter without relating an incident concerning a Christian friend of mine. One day he was relaxing in the office cafeteria during his lunch break, doing a crossword puzzle. He came to number 12 across: three letters, beginning with 'G'. The clue: 'Spirit'. Without hesitation he wrote 'GOD'.

Soon he realised that some vertical words didn't seem to fit. After tussling for a while he gave up and passed over the newspaper to a workmate who liked a crossword challenge.

'What on earth made you put "GOD" for 12 across?' asked the man. 'It's "GIN!"'

Now some would say my friend was a bit naïve. For myself, I prefer to see him as a man whose mind was filled with thoughts of God and wholesomeness. If someone could come along with a ladle and dip it into your mind, what sort of thoughts would they pull out?

The choice is entirely yours.

Chapter 8 NOTES

[1] See 2 Timothy 3:16; 2 Peter 1:21

[2] Psalm 119:15

[3] Colossians 3:16

[4] 1 Timothy 4:7

[5] John 14:26

[6] Philippians 4:8

[7] Psalm 1:2

Thinking your way to change

'People don't change.'

So states an old adage based upon generations of observation of human nature. And in general it is true. The sour and embittered youth grows into a sour and embittered old man. The teenage girl who plays off one parent against the other can be found playing the same manipulative games with the nurses in the old folks' home when she is ninety.

But thank God, in Christ genuine change is possible. And I don't mean simply the transformation that will overtake us when Jesus returns at the end of the age. Then, to be sure, 'the trumpet will sound, the dead will be raised imperishable, and *we will be changed'.*[1] No matter how unlike Jesus we may be at present, 'we know that when he appears, we shall be like him'.[2]

But happily, we don't have to wait until then to get started. Visible change into the likeness of Christ can, and should, begin here and now, this side of his return: 'We...*are being* transformed into his likeness'.[3]

Metamorphosis

'Transformed'—now there's an interesting word. The Greek word Paul uses gives us the English *metamorphosis*, the process by which a dull, brown caterpillar, for example, becomes a gorgeous butterfly. Paul is saying that we Christians are undergoing a radical transformation, sprouting, not wings like the butterfly, but Christ-like character.

In changing us this way, God is doing what he has always intended doing: obtaining a people who are *like himself,* people who bear the true family likeness. Adam and Eve were created that way, 'in the image of God',[4] and were commanded to multiply and fill the earth. But sin quickly came in to spoil the picture and fill the earth with sinful, mixed-up people instead.

Then came Jesus, the Son of God. He undid the devil's work. Just as sinful Adam had headed up a family of sinful, Adam-like people, Jesus died and rose again to become head of a family of Christ-like, godly people—a people, incidentally, who are still destined to fill the earth one day, according to God's original plan.

Catching up

You entered this new family when you became a believer in Jesus. But as you have probably noticed (and if you haven't, you can be sure your friends have), you did not become perfect overnight.

Here, it is vital to distinguish between your *standing* in God's eyes and your present actual *state.* In God's eyes you are already viewed as perfect 'in Christ' (to use Paul's favourite expression). The perfection of Jesus has been put to your account, just as your sin was put to his account and paid off in full when he died on the cross. Your day-by-day state of godliness, however, lags behind. It has to catch up, and this is a lifelong process.

You may remember God's warning to Adam about eating the forbidden fruit in Eden: 'When you eat of it,' he warned, 'you will surely die'.[5] Adam ate, but did he die on the spot?

No, at least not physically. On a spiritual level, death took place instantly, but the practical and physical outworking of it took many years to catch up. This same process operates in reverse when you become a Christian. You become instantly perfect in Christ as far as your acceptance with God is concerned, but it takes many years for the outworking of it in character-development to catch up. That process is in operation right now; you *are being* transformed'.

The renewing of the mind

But no way is this something you just sit back and let happen. God expects you to take the process seriously by co-operating with him in it. That is why Paul, once again using the word 'metamorphosis', urges us, 'Do not conform any longer to the pattern of this world, but *be transformed...*'⁶ Here, it is an order, a command.

'And how exactly do I obey it?' you may well ask.

The answer, given by Paul in the very same verse, could not be clearer: 'Be transformed *by the renewing of your mind.'*

Now you can see why a sound, renewed mind is so vital: it is the key to transformation—to character-change and growth in godliness.

Change from the inside out

Christianity, you must understand, was never intended to be a veneer of smiles, charity, churchgoing and good works, masking a still-sinful heart and mind. On the contrary, the change that God intends is programmed to take effect *from the inside out.* At the core of your being is what the Bible usually calls your *heart.* This refers, not to your blood-pump, but to your essential nature. 'The heart is deceitful above all things and beyond cure,' complained Jeremiah (17:9), referring, of course, to the natural, sinful heart which we all once had. Its bias was evil. We were literally 'rotten to the core'.

But another great prophet, Ezekiel, foretold a time when God would perform 'heart surgery'. 'I will remove from them their heart of stone,' God declared, 'and give them a heart of flesh. Then they will follow my decrees and be careful to keep my laws. They will be my people, and I will be their God'.[7]

You and I live, as Christians, in the good of that promise. We have a new heart, one programmed to please God or, to use Jeremiah's expression—because computer programming wasn't around in his day—a heart on which God's law is written. Our bias is now one of godliness. Wonderful!

Mind and will

So much for the heart, which is the core of your being. Then there is the *mind.* Your mind receives data (we are into computers again) from two directions. First, from your new heart, which feeds it godly impulses. And second, from the world around you, by way of your senses and the 'gates' we referred to earlier.

The godly impulses are strong. The powerful Holy Spirit within you 'knows the thoughts of God'[8] and releases those thoughts into your mind. As a result, it is no exaggeration for us to claim, along with Paul, that 'we have the mind of Christ'.[9]

Closely linked to your mind is your *will*—the apparatus by which you make decisions. This, too, is directly influenced by God from the inside: 'It is God who is at work in you, both to *will* and to work for his good pleasure'.[10]

In view of all this, we can never complain that God has left us to struggle on alone. He has changed our heart, given us a godly bias, placed within us his Holy Spirit to feed his very own thoughts into our minds, and begun to work upon our wills. What an incentive to co-operate with him!

And co-operate we must. If we allow the attitudes of the world to flow in unchecked through the gateways of our minds, the godly impulses coming from deep within us will be neutralised, at least as far as their character-forming power is concerned. Instead of becoming more like the Lord we shall remain conformed 'to the pattern of this world' or, as J.B. Phillips puts it, 'squeezed into its mould'.

Digging for silver

What, then, can we do? How, in view of the fact that God is so graciously at work in us, can we play our part and *'work out* [our] own salvation'?[11]

That expression 'work out' gives us a clue. The same Greek word was used by Strabo, a writer in the first century BC, in connection with some silver mines in Spain. He describes how the Romans 'worked out' the silver from the mines. The land was in their possession, but the ore lay hidden beneath the surface. Left underground, it was of no value. If it was to grace people's lives in the shape of silver ornaments and jewellery it had to be 'worked out'. Hard work was necessary in digging down to the veins of silver ore, extracting it, bringing it to the surface, smelting it and forming it into beautiful objects.

Deep within you is a mine of far greater wealth than silver. The very life and character of God is there, a treasure of immense value. But it must not be kept underground; you need to 'work it out'.

How? By allowing it first to control your mind. From there it will automatically work its way to the surface of your life in visible godliness of character, displayed in the way you speak and act. That way, the beauty of Christ in you will be evident for all to see. The change in you will astound them, causing some of them, no doubt, to turn to Christ themselves.

Mind: the key to character

The key is the mind. If you let godless data pour in indiscriminately to become the dominant influence, your mind will become a buffer, preventing the influences of your new heart from touching your outward character and behaviour. On the other hand, by giving preference to righteous thinking you can release your mind's power to shape your character for God.

There is a principle here: *whatever dominates a person's mind will dictate their character.* Worldly thought patterns will keep them worldly. Godly thought patterns will make them godly. 'As he *thinks* within himself, so he *is*'.[12]

For you to co-operate with God in this business of changing, therefore, you must *make a decision to let your mind be governed by the godly influences from within* rather than by the worldly ones from without. The Bible says, 'Those who live in accordance with the Spirit *have their minds set* on what the Spirit desires... The *mind controlled by the Spirit* is life and peace'.[13] The meaning is plain: the key to a Christ-like character, one marked by life and peace, is a mind 'controlled by the Spirit'.

The right wavelength

And how do you place your mind under his control? By deliberately *setting* it on what he desires, just as you might choose to set your radio to a particular wavelength. Tune your mind to wholesome thinking.

In a similar passage, noted earlier, Paul urges: *'Set your minds on* things above, not on earthly things…since you have taken off your old self with its practices and have put on the new self, which *is being renewed in knowledge in the image of its Creator'*.[14] That's it: we are being changed into our Creator's image. How? By a renewal of knowledge (or mind). And how do we co-operate? By choosing to set our minds on the things of God.

An old proverb states: 'Sow a thought, reap an action; sow an action, reap a habit; sow a habit, reap a character; sow a character, reap a destiny.' The moral is clear: if you want to fulfil your destiny of being a person in the image of God, sow the right thoughts.

Ruts in the road

In closing this section, let us return briefly to what we said earlier about our being creatures of habit, for there are habits of thinking as well as of speech and behaviour.

From the time you were born, right up to the time you put your faith in Jesus, you thought in worldly ways. The world's ideas and attitudes rested easily in your thinking. You could liken your thought patterns to the ruts formed in a farm track by the farmer's four-by-four. The softening effect of the rain and the daily trips of the four-by-four, combined with the passage of time, have caused the track to become deeply scarred. In fact, the ruts now act like tram-lines; the farmer can take his hands off the wheel, confident that the ruts will steer him down to the farmhouse.

That is how your pre-conversion thought patterns were established. For years, the ceaseless traffic of unrighteous thinking travelled the length and breadth of your mind. Ruts were quickly formed. Worldly thoughts fitted those ruts exactly and drove comfortably up and down. They probably still do.

Under new management

Now suppose there is a change of management. The farmer sells up and moves off the premises. A new owner moves in. The new man doesn't use a four-by-four for his trips into town; he drives a Mercedes saloon. What a struggle he has on his way up the track! Why? Because the wheels of his car do not fit the ruts. He has to grip the steering-wheel tightly to keep the vehicle on course.

That is your problem exactly. Godly thoughts do not fit the ruts in your mind, especially when you first become a Christian. It is far easier to let go of righteous thoughts and go back to the old variety that fit the well-worn ruts so much better. But that would be to go down-market and settle for less than the best, wouldn't it?

The farmer decided not to go down-market. So, tough work though it was, especially at the beginning, he persevered with his Mercedes. Gradually it got easier to drive up and down the track because *new ruts slowly began to be formed—ones that matched the wheels on his car.* Eventually the new ruts replaced the old ones completely, his driving became easy and a visitor's four-by-four was now the vehicle to have a rough ride.

Stay with it!

Persevere with your pursuit of godliness. Set your mind steadfastly upon it. Give the new management a chance. At first the going will be tough, but gradually you will find the old thought patterns giving way to new, godly, ones. Righteous thoughts will feel increasingly at home and, eventually, it will be thoughts of the old variety that have a rough ride.

This is the way to real and lasting change. By altering your patterns of thought you affect your patterns of behaviour. God has done everything possible to help you; don't opt out of your part in the deal.

Chapter 9 NOTES

[1] 1 Corinthians 15:52

[2] 1 John 3:2

[3] 2 Corinthians 3:18

[4] Genesis 1:27

[5] Genesis 2:17

[6] Romans 12:2

[7] Ezekiel 11:19-20

[8] 1 Corinthians 2:11-12

[9] 1 Corinthians 2:16

[10] Philippians 2:13 NASB

[11] Philippians 2:12-13

[12] Proverbs 23:7 NASB

[13] Romans 8:5-6

[14] See Colossians 3:2, 5-10

Chapter 10

The power of imagination

People in every generation have recognised the power of the mind. Marcus Aurelius observed in the second century, 'Our life is what our thoughts make it.' And in the present century, Norman Vincent Peale has stated, 'Change your thoughts and you change your world.' All that these observers have done is to grasp a basic principle that God himself built into humanity and which finds clear expression in the pages of Scripture.

Much of our thinking is done in pictures. We have a cinema screen inside our minds called the *imagination*, and on it we view one episode after another, films in which we ourselves invariably play the leading role. Without question the imagination is one of the most influential aspects of the mind. It could well have been this that the writer of Proverbs was thinking of when he wrote, 'As he thinks within himself, so he is'.[1]

Let's consider one or two case histories of individuals in Scripture and see how their imagination shaped their lives.

Dreams of greatness

Take Joseph, for example. His imagination was affected for life by a God-given dream he had at the age of seventeen, in which he saw himself as a leader.[2] He imagined people bowing before him in awe and respect. Though circumstances seemed for years to militate against its realisation, the dream never left him and in due course it was amazingly fulfilled. I have written about this in my book *Dead Dreams Can Live!*

Like you, Joseph regularly viewed imagination-films. I don't mean that he went into wild flights of fantasy based on pride or wishful thinking, like James Thurber's famous character, Walter Mitty. No, his imagination was fuelled by a revelation from God. Joseph reviewed his films daily and saw them become reality. This was no coincidence. His dream—the moving, talking pictures he saw on the screen of his imagination—wasn't some detached feature unrelated to what eventually took place. Far from it. It had a positive role to play in that it actually helped shape the reality.

That is how imagination works. God has invested it with the power to bring into existence the pictures it projects.

Drawn to a drunkard

Bill Gothard tells of a girl who suffered at the hands of an alcoholic father, a brute of a man who, under the influence of drink, inflicted violence on her and his wife and regularly smashed up the home. From an early age the girl determined that she would never befriend, let alone marry, any man who was a drinker. Etched permanently on to the screen of her imagination was the picture of a violent drunkard.

In due course she became friendly with a young man and the relationship blossomed into romance. Even at that early stage he used to drink heavily at times. During the period of their engagement he once or twice beat her up. Nevertheless, she went on to marry him and ended up living a life that was a carbon copy of the situation she had vowed to avoid.

How on earth could such a thing happen? Simply because,

day and night, her imagination was filled with a picture of a drunken man, a picture which irrevocably drew her into the reality of what it portrayed.

'But wait a minute,' I can hear you protesting. 'She had that mental picture as the thing she wanted to *avoid*, not as the thing she desired.'

That is no doubt true. But the fact is, the imagination simply doesn't work according to that kind of logic. Whatever it portrays has a powerful tendency to draw us into itself, often overriding other mental factors. Maybe this girl's case was extreme, but it illustrates the immense power of the imagination.

Grasshoppers

The ten unbelieving Israelite spies who reconnoitred the Promised Land for Moses[3] learned the same lesson. When they saw the gigantic Nephilim their hearts sank—how could they possibly hope to defeat such an enemy? What they should have done, *on the strength of God's promise,* was to imagine themselves cutting the giants down and encouraging one another with, 'The taller they are, the harder they fall!' The Bible calls that faith. Instead, they imagined the huge fellows pointing down at them in derision and jesting with each other, 'Do you want to stamp on that grasshopper, or shall I?' That is called unbelief.

Their dejected report to Moses on their return was, 'We can't attack those people... We seemed like grasshoppers in our own eyes, and we looked the same to them'.[4] These men never became residents of the Promised Land; they died in the desert.

Notice the phrase 'we seemed like grasshoppers *in our own*

eyes'. People who picture themselves as grasshoppers on the screen of their imagination end up acting like grasshoppers in reality: the enemy shouts 'Boo!' and they jump.

By contrast, recall the poor woman with the haemorrhage described in Matthew 9. Having tried every remedy without success, she pinned her hopes on Jesus. Scripture records that she said to herself, 'If I only touch his cloak, I will be healed' (v21). She was visualising the event, imagining herself pushing forward through the crowd, reaching out her hand and touching the edge of Jesus' cloak. What she visualised spurred her to action and so it came to pass.

We can call it visualisation, imagination or whatever. Jesus called it faith. Regardless of what we call it, it is something to emulate. It gets results.

The sad case of Saul

Centuries earlier, Saul had become Israel's first king. From a good family and favoured with striking good looks, not to mention specially-conferred prophetic gifts, Saul seemed to have the makings of a fine ruler. But his reign ended in disgrace and disaster.

The reasons are many and complex, not least among them his downright disobedience to the Lord. In addition, he was bloated with pride, especially after taking the throne. But he seems also to have had an imagination problem: a poor self-image. Pride and a poor self-image may seem strange bedfellows but, oddly enough, the two are often found together.

Saul's behaviour poses many questions. Why, for instance, did he hold back from his uncle the thrilling news of his selection for kingship?[5] Why, when the big moment came for him to be publicly presented to the nation, did he run away and hide among the baggage?[6] Why, later on, did he develop a persecution complex?[7] And why was he always holding a spear (a weapon which doubled as a royal sceptre), even when sitting at home and eating at table?[8] All these factors point to a man who was deeply insecure. His 'pride', in that case, would be the exaggerated words and actions of a man intent on making his mark while inwardly lacking the confidence to do it.

The prophet Samuel made a telling remark. In saying to Saul, 'You were once *small in your own eyes*',[9] he was referring, I suggest, not just to Saul's modesty or the ordinariness of his family background, but to his pitifully inadequate view of himself. It is easy to imagine the kind of pictures Saul watched on the screen in his mind. He saw himself as failing, as the object of dislike, as bungling. And that, of course, is exactly what he became—because that is how God, in his wisdom, has fixed the human machine to operate.

Thoughts projected and reflected

Saul's sad story reveals another aspect of the self-image business: *how we see ourselves dictates how other people see us and treat us.*

It is no surprise to read that Saul wasn't well received by all the people when, after chickening out of his public presentation, he was eventually found, dusted down and stood up on the podium. While the majority dutifully shouted, 'Long live the king!', some 'despised him and brought him no gifts'.[10]

I wonder if some of these detected in his eyes a lack of self-confidence and thought to themselves, 'Why should we put our confidence in this man if he hasn't even got confidence in himself?' That is how it works. In some indefinable way we project our view of ourselves to others, who then reflect it back to us by treating us the way we regard ourselves.

This used to be a problem for me, even after being born again and filled with the Holy Spirit. The outworking of change, remember, takes time. Having a pretty poor opinion of my own worth, I assumed that others would not want to be around me. And they didn't—my poor self-image made sure of that.

The walking wet blanket

My imagination would work overtime when it came to social gatherings. I would imagine, for instance, turning up at someone's house for the housegroup meeting—late, because the phone had rung just as I was going out. As I hung my coat up in the hallway, I would look timidly at the lounge door. It was closed, but from behind it came the sound of happy laughter and conversation from the rest of the group. How I wished I didn't have to go in!

I turned the handle and walked in. For a second or two, which seemed like an eternity, I was framed in the doorway, with all eyes upon me as people paused in their chatter to see who was coming in. How I hated that!

They were all smiling pleasantly, but inside they were thinking, 'Oh dear, *he's* turned up—old misery guts, the walking wet blanket.'

Then someone would politely make room for me to sit down and would remark how nice it was to see me. But inwardly he was thinking, 'What a pain! Now I'm stuck sitting next to this unsociable twit for the rest of the evening!'

All this took place in glorious Technicolor on the screen of my imagination. The tragedy is that, for the reason I just explained, the negative way I imagined myself began to dictate the way people treated me. That, of course, confirmed my worst suspicions about myself. It was a vicious circle, and I actually—inevitably—became the kind of person I imagined myself to be.

Be a film producer!

Maybe you are beginning to identify with some of this—with the principle if not with the details—and are wondering what to do about it. How can this imagination of yours, with all its power to shape your future, be brought under control?

The answer is simple: *you must become a film producer!*

Put on a new programme at your mental cinema, screening self-produced films in which you figure as the person *God* declares you to be in his Word. You can do it. In fact, you must—you're responsible, remember?

And what *does* God declare you to be? An individual chosen in Christ Jesus before the creation of the world;[11] a child of none less than God himself, and greatly loved;[12] a person through whom the Holy Spirit works for the blessing of others;[13] someone triumphant in all circumstances[14]—the list could go on and on. Create imagination-films that portray you in this positive, biblical way, and that is what you will increasingly become.

Let's be clear here. I am not talking at all about some New Age mind-control technique that pride can feed on to make you into a ruthless self-seeker. I am assuming you have been to the cross and died there with Jesus,[15] that you have been 'united with him...in his death'.[16] I am taking it for granted that your old self has been buried and that a new you has sprung to life by the power of God. If so, are you, like Lazarus, simply wanting to see the grave-clothes removed so that you can enjoy your new life in Christ to the full, for his glory? Then what I am saying is for you. And it is not New Age, it is New Testament.

Reshaping the old movies

Begin by adapting some of the old, negative films. Here is the amended version of the one I described just now.

As I hung up my coat in the hallway and heard the sounds of laughter and conversation through the lounge door, a smile came over my lips. I paused with my hand on the handle and said to myself, 'Those folk in there have no idea what a blessing on two legs is about to walk in among them. They probably thought I wasn't coming tonight, but they're in for a lovely surprise!'

I opened the door. There I stood, framed in the doorway with a big smile on my face as all eyes turned to see who was coming in.

'Oh great, Dave's here!' Some said it out loud, others just thought it, but they all meant it—I know they did, because I'm the producer and I made the film that way. Then someone moved along on the sofa and invited me to sit down, thinking, 'Fantastic! It's great to have Dave next to me to chat to.'

It took time, and there were other factors involved, too, but little by little, as I persisted in exercising faith by taking my imagination in hand, I became a different kind of person altogether. And now it is permanent. I have simply changed. You can change, too. But do not expect it to happen over-night. All change takes time, but surely if anything is worth persisting with, this must be it.

As you train your imagination and bring it into line with the Word of God you will often be surprised suddenly to find yourself looking at the old negative films again. A phantom projectionist, hired by the enemy, has removed your latest positive production from the machine and stuck the old one back in. Well, you know by now what to do with intruders. Then put the right film on show again. Feed your mind and imagination—and mould your character—with the truths of God's Word.

Your faith-image

In the very next verse after the one in which Paul mentions the renewing of the mind he says, 'Do not think of yourself more highly than you ought, but rather think of yourself with sober judgment, in accordance with the measure of faith God has given you'.[17]

Pride has no place in God's kingdom. In this chapter I have not been encouraging you to become a big-head. If you are that already—like one young man I met who claimed he was an apostle, a prophet, an evangelist, a pastor and a teacher all rolled into one—then you need to sober down a bit in your self-estimation, as Paul suggests.

My observation of Christians today, however, leads me to believe that many of them have the opposite problem, which is why I have tackled the imagination question in some detail.

Whatever your situation, Paul's statement in the latter part of the verse holds good: your self-image is a matter of *faith*. Faith in the plain statements of Scripture as to who you are in Christ. Faith that the Lord who chose you, called you and saved you did so to make you a blessing on two legs, taking the light of his presence with you wherever you go.

Believe it. Think it. Imagine it. *Be* it!

Chapter 10 NOTES

[1] Proverbs 23:7 NASB

[2] See Genesis 37

[3] Numbers 13

[4] v31, 33

[5] 1 Samuel 10:16

[6] 1 Samuel 10:20-23

[7] 1 Samuel 22:6-8

[8] 1 Samuel 18:10; 19:9; 20:33; 22:6; 26:7

[9] 1 Samuel 15:17

[10] 1 Samuel 10:24, 27

[11] Ephesians 1:4

[12] 1 John 3:1

[13] 1 Corinthians 12:7

[14] Romans 8:37

[15] Galatians 2:20

[16] Romans 6:5

[17] Romans 12:3

Chapter 11

A mind at peace

'Peace of mind—yours for a small monthly payment.' Only in the promotional blurb of some insurance company could such a claim be made.

Within the narrow limits of the insurance world the claim is probably fair. The peace of mind most of us are looking for, however, must be far wider-ranging than that. We live in an age of uncertainty. We need a mental peace that will enable us to cope adequately with the unpredictable demands of marriage (or singleness), child-raising, finance, work, health, the possibility of redundancy and violence, and the innumerable decisions we have to make each week.

In Chapter One we reviewed some of the pressures under which we live as citizens of the twenty-first century. Is it really possible, in such circumstances, to enjoy a mind at peace?

Happily, it is. God himself—Father, Son and Holy Spirit —is the guarantee of it. The Father to whom we have submitted our thinking is called 'the God of peace';[1] Jesus our Lord is the 'Prince of Peace';[2] and 'the mind controlled by the Spirit is life and peace'.[3]

So let's take a closer look at the triune God's provision for handling anxiety.

Anxious? Then stop it!

It may sound trite, but the Bible's answer to anxiety is the same answer it gives to both sin and doubt: *stop it!*

'Do not be anxious about anything,' says Paul bluntly.[4] It is an order, and an order, as we have seen, presupposes our ability—with God's help—to obey it. Simply refuse, then, to entertain anxiety. Make your mind a 'no go' area to worries. Be vigilant at each gateway of the mind and turn back each anxious thought, seeing through the fancy dress in which some arrive. They usually turn up masquerading as realism or common sense, promising to do you good, while in truth they are saboteurs intent on wrecking whatever peace of mind you already enjoyed. So take a hard line.

Counter measures

Then, remembering the danger of creating a spiritual vacuum, the next step is to see what positive alternative to worry Scripture presents. The second half of Paul's injunction quoted above supplies it: 'Do not be anxious about anything, *but in everything, by prayer and petition, with thanksgiving, present your requests to God.'*

Every difficulty we face, every worry-laden situation, is a challenge to faith.[5] It is packed with both potential misery and potential blessing. We must decide to ignore the misery and go for the blessing. But like the silver in Strabo's silver mines, the blessing requires certain steps to be taken if it is to be 'worked out', and Paul outlines them for us here.

There are two basic steps. Begin with *thanksgiving*. I don't mean a ridiculous, super-spiritual cry of, 'Oh thank you, Lord, that I'm likely to be out of work from next month, with no money to pay the mortgage. It's what I always wanted!' No, we give thanks, first, for the fact that God, who loves us, is in control and that the devil cannot do anything to us without his permission. Then we give thanks that here is yet another opportunity to trust God, to see him act on our behalf and to grow in faith and character.

The second step, after thanksgiving, is to *'present your requests to God'* in prayer. Request him to give you wisdom in the situation, and he will.[6] Ask him to give you a clear mind and sensitivity to the voice of the Holy Spirit, so that you can make whatever decisions are necessary. Ask him to take the weight of the situation upon his own broad shoulders.

God's own peace

Thanksgiving and prayer will rarely be one-off steps. As long as the worry-promoting circumstances persist, keep taking these two tablets. As you do, you will enter into the good of one of the Bible's most blessed promises: *'The peace of God, which transcends all understanding, will guard your hearts and your minds in Christ Jesus'.*[7]

We are not talking here about peace *with* God. You have that already, I trust, by faith in Jesus.[8] We are talking about the peace *of* God—the peace that God himself enjoys and dispenses to his children. Can you imagine the Lord biting his fingernails with worry? What a ridiculous idea! Well, he promises that if you will just meet the simple conditions of thanksgiving and prayer, he will infuse into you his very own peace.

He *doesn't* say that he will take away the anxiety-promoting circumstances immediately, but he *will* give you his peace in the very midst of them. What a wonderful experience this is! I have known it myself, many times, and I have spoken to other Christians who, amid circumstances that would make an unbeliever sick with worry, have declared, 'It's amazing, but I feel real peace in the situation.'

'Yes, but how exactly does this work?' you may ask. That will always be a fruitless line of enquiry, because the peace of God *'transcends understanding'*. In other words, it operates at a higher level than rational thought or logical analysis. It takes no account of the worry-factor that the natural mind is so prone to dwell upon. All you have to do is let it take over. Your part of the deal is thanksgiving and prayer; God does the rest.

Paul explains to his Philippian friends what the peace of God will do: it will, he says, *'guard your hearts and your minds'*. In other words, at times of exceptional pressure on your mind, the peace of God is sent to reinforce your own defences at the border posts of your thinking.

Divine reinforcements

A man of God was once being hunted by his enemies. During the night they surrounded Dothan, the little town where he lay asleep. Next morning, his servant nearly died of fright when he peered over the town wall and saw the surrounding hordes. He rushed to tell Elisha, his master, who, instead of worrying, received the grim news with amazing calm.

'Don't be afraid,' he said to his trembling servant. 'Those who are with us are more than those who are with them.'

The servant found that hard to understand. The enemy forces far outnumbered the total population of Dothan. Then his master asked God to open the servant's eyes supernaturally to see what he himself already saw by the eye of faith: 'the hills full of horses and chariots of fire all round Elisha'—divine warriors guarding the man of God.[9] Supernatural defences are yours, too, when surrounding worries threaten to break through the barriers and smash up your mind. God has promised it, and he will no doubt provide you with opportunity to experience it.

The stronger can guard the weaker, but never vice versa. Who would expect a little five-year-old to guard his father? The fact that this 'peace of God', according to the Bible, can 'guard your mind and heart' indicates that it is far more powerful than you are. Enjoy it. Summoned by thanksgiving and prayer, it comes as your personal bodyguard—or should I say *mind*guard?—when the pressure to worry is on.

The decision-making threat

If anxiety is a threat for some, others are pressured by *the need to make decisions.*

Those who suffer worst in this respect may ponder for ages which shirt to put on in a morning, or whether to have marmalade or strawberry jam on their toast. When asked, 'Tea or coffee?' they reply, 'Oh, either,' leaving the decision to someone else. Anything to avoid being decisive.

Fortunately, most people can handle such trivial decisions without too much trouble. They can come under pressure, however, when facing more important ones like moving house, changing jobs, disciplining their children, swapping the car or joining a trade union. The need for a decision can feel like an enormous weight pressing down on the mind, paralysing even further the little decision-making ability they have.

How, then, can we make wise decisions?

Remember, first of all, that *God* is decisive. He never paces the room in a mental quandary or sits around with a glazed look in his eye while things collapse all around him for lack of action. No. He says, 'Let there be... Let us make...' and then gets on with it.[10] If you are his child, partaking of his divine nature, you should expect to be the same. Indecision is largely a habit—one that belongs to the old, pre-Christian life. This particular rut in the road may be very deep, but even the most indecisive person can change, given time and a willingness to co-operate with God.

Decisiveness is, in fact, one of the major products of the renewed mind. 'Be transformed by the renewing of your mind,' urges Paul, adding, *'Then you will be able to test and approve what God's will is'*.[11] That is what you want, isn't it—to know God's will when you face a decision? So how can you do it?

Options

Begin by surveying the options.

It may help you to write them down. Think carefully about each one and its likely consequences. First consider all the *possible* consequences, then the *probable* ones. Then recognise that, in an imperfect world, there probably isn't one perfect answer. This realisation—especially vital if you are a natural nit-picker or perfectionist—will save you from looking long and hard for something that doesn't exist. Whatever option you choose will have its drawbacks.

At this stage you may want to ask some qualified person or persons for advice. Ask them to give reasons for their opinions so that you can add these to your own considerations.

Above all, ask the Lord for *his* advice, remembering that

'those who live in accordance with the Spirit have their minds set on what the Spirit desires'.[12] Normally you won't need to spend days or weeks in prayer to hear from God. Having asked, trust him to work in you by his Spirit to lead you to a wise decision.

The inner referee

One way he does this is by means of the 'peace-referee'. You will find this in Colossians 3:15, where Paul counsels, 'Let the peace of Christ *rule* in your hearts.'

The word 'rule' here isn't the usual one. In fact the Greek word behind it occurs only once in the whole New Testament—right here. Its meaning is 'to act as umpire or referee'. We could therefore translate Paul's statement: *'Let the peace of Christ act as referee in your hearts.'*

What does a referee do? He monitors the game on the field and makes decisions in the course of play. He is a decision-maker. In this case the referee is 'the peace of Christ'. Compare it to a deep pool of water inside you. While its normal condition is to be as calm as the proverbial millpond, its surface smooth and undisturbed, occasionally it is disturbed by splashes and ripples, as if someone had thrown in a stone.

Suppose you are surveying the various options that lie open to you as you face an important decision. When you think about Option A, the peace-pool is disturbed. You feel all churned up inside by some inexplicable source of unrest. But Option B has the opposite effect: as soon as you let your mind dwell upon it, the ripples fade away and the surface of the peace-pool becomes as smooth as a mirror. In that case, go for Option B. Often, logic alone will favour a different approach and you will find yourself trying to shout down the persistent voice of the inner referee. He is a gentleman, and if you insist hard enough he will let you have your own way—at a cost. Don't do it.

We have seen earlier how vital it is to submit the mind to the will of God, which operates at a deeper level than mere reason. This 'peace of Christ' is part of his provision to help you make decisions, an inner referee who knows God's rules from back to front and lets you know when you are about to play a foul. Don't ignore him. *'Let* the peace of Christ rule....'

Facing major decisions inevitably causes us all a degree of nervousness as we realise how vital it is to get it right. This nervousness is not the same as the disturbing of the peace-pool caused by considering a bad option. I can't tell you how to spot the difference, but you will know when the time comes. Being able to detect it readily is a sign of growing spiritual maturity. Expect things to become clear as you pray.

'I will!'

So you have now surveyed your options, considering the likely consequences of each one. You have taken advice. You have committed your way to the Lord and taken note of the peace-referee. Now it is time to choose.

Make your choice. State your 'I will'. Say to yourself, 'OK, this is what I'll do.'

Then do it! Be like the prodigal son who, having said to himself, *'I will* set out and go back to my father,' promptly 'got up and *went* to his father'.[13]

You may think this is the end of it—the decision made and the action begun—but it isn't. How many times, I wonder, did the prodigal pause on the road home and ask himself,

'Am I doing the right thing? What chance do I stand of any kind of welcome from my father after the way I've treated him? Was I having a brainstorm when I decided to go back home?'

You will face similar doubts about your own decision. Ignore them. You considered all the possible consequences of your action when you surveyed your options, so don't waste time going over the same ground again. Put your energy instead into implementing the decision. Setbacks, weariness and fear are normal at this stage. Stay with your decision and work it through. In a word, be *single-minded*. Chronic indecision—called in the Bible double-mindedness—will destabilise not only your mind but your whole life and future, because a 'double-minded man' is 'unstable in *all* he does'.[14]

Peace in the storm

I once saw a picture entitled 'Peace'. It wasn't a calm country landscape with sunshine and grazing cows or someone taking a nap. It portrayed a raging storm on a rocky coast. Violent winds whipped across the foam, drawing the waters up into enormous waves that thundered down onto the rocks. Driving rain, mingled with fierce sea-spray, struck diagonally across the picture.

Then after a moment or two of taking in this violent scene, my eye was drawn to one corner of the picture. In a crevice of a rock stood a small sea-bird. Sheltered there in the midst of storm, wind, rain and crashing waves, it enjoyed peace.

That is exactly what you can expect. Let life throw up all the opposition it can muster. Let worry and anxiety threaten. Let major decisions stand towering above you. Not by removal from it all but in the very midst of it, God has made provision for you to enjoy a mind at peace.

Chapter 11 NOTES

[1] 1 Thessalonians 5:23

[2] Isaiah 9:6

[3] Romans 8:6

[4] Philippians 4:6

[5] See James 1:2-4

[6] James 1:5

[7] Philippians 4:7

[8] Romans 5:1

[9] 2 Kings 6:8-17

[10] Genesis 1:3, 26

[11] Romans 12:2

[12] Romans 8:5

[13] Luke 15:18, 20

[14] James 1:8

Beating depression

Few people can claim never to have had a bout of depression.

Even great Bible characters experienced it, people like Jonah, Elijah, Peter, Moses, Job, Jeremiah and David. In fact, depression is so common that we could call it the mental and emotional equivalent of the common cold.

The symptoms are well-known. You feel desperately unhappy, often for no apparent reason. You tend to lose interest in food, sex, personal appearance and other people. Often you can't sleep. Everything seems too much effort. The future looks bleak, while, in the present, worry and fear are your constant companions. You fluctuate between being sad and angry, weepy and irritable. You may be physically unwell. In your abysmal despair you may even contemplate suicide.

There are different degrees of depression, of course, and only in severe cases would a person experience all the symptoms just described.

Prevention is always better than cure. I can assure you that if you put into practice the principles outlined in this book so far, you will be well on the way to a healthy mind that is strongly resistant to depression.

Some common causes

Let's take a quick look at some of its many causes and highlight the truths that, if lived out in faith, can resist it.

First, there are *hard circumstances*. It may be bereavement, disappointment, financial setback or some other loss or trage-dy. Such trials are normal and can be turned around for blessing. Take some time to read what James has to say on the subject (James 1:2-4).

There is *the burden of past failure*. Thoughts can storm Memory Gate and invade your mind with depressive results. But God, you will recall, has chosen to forget your past fail-ures and it is your privilege to do the same.

Depressing material can reach us by way of *books, the news media, music, films and scaremongering political propaganda*. Insist on feeding your mind only on edifying material and put your trust in God, who holds the future in his hands.

The belief that you are making only very *slow progress towards godliness* can plunge you into despair, making you want to give up trying. Remember that there is no such thing as instant character-change. It takes time for the ruts in the road to be re-formed. Stay with it.

When major pressures are on you, *loneliness* can aggravate the situation. Recall how Brian overcame his garden problem. Forge close relationships with Christian friends and ask for help when you need it.

A poor self-image is guaranteed to pull you down. Keep your eyes on God's opinion of your unique worth as declared in Scripture. Project the right films on to the screen of your imagination.

Anxiety and *the need to make decisions* can lead to depression.

Look again at the guidelines in the last chapter and put them into practice right away.

More causes

In addition to the above, we can pinpoint *physical* causes. Glandular malfunctions, chemical deficiencies, low blood sugar or a hormone imbalance may be to blame. If pre-menstrual tension (caused by hormonal changes) is a recurring problem, be sensible and plan heavy responsibilities for a different time of the month. Equally, the physical cause could be a poor diet or lack of sleep. Hopefully in your case it won't be alcohol or drug abuse. Medical testing will normally reveal if the cause of depression comes into this category. It can then be treated accordingly.

Don't hesitate to accept medication if it is prescribed. Some Christians shy away from this, as if there is some dreadful shame involved in even admitting that a mental problem exists, let alone in taking medication for it.

We live in an age of medical expertise. If your eyesight is not what it was, you don't hesitate to have an eye test, accept the optician's prescription and get spectacles. It is no different with depression caused by a chemical imbalance in your body. Rejoice that treatment is available and take advantage of it without shame, rejecting the super-spiritual foolishness that says having recourse to medicine shows a lack of faith. Oliver Cromwell famously told his troops, 'Trust in God and keep your powder dry.' Nehemiah records that, when he and his fellow-builders came under threat of attack, 'We prayed to our God and posted a guard.' They saw no incompatibility between faith and sensible practical action. Neither should you.

Childhood experiences can sometimes catch up with us and

trigger depression. If your parents had over-high expectations of you in school or college, for instance, your constant struggles to please them may have drained your reservoir of self-worth. The emotional trauma of seeing your father and mother go through a divorce may also have delayed-action effects. Worse still, you may have been neglected or have suffered abuse, psychological, physical or sexual, possibly at the hands of those closest to you and whom you thus trusted most. Such a betrayal of childhood trust can be devastating.

In this case we are probably looking at a stronghold of the mind (possibly the subconscious mind), which will need discerning and demolishing in the way we described in Chapter Six.

Handling guilt

The cause may, of course, be just plain *guilt*. You may have committed a crime that was never discovered. You may have secretly abused a child or yielded to some other sexual perversion—most likely before becoming a Christian, though possibly after.

David knew all about the effects, both mental and physical, of hiding sin: 'When I kept silent, my bones wasted away through my groaning all day long. For day and night your hand was heavy upon me; my strength was sapped as in the heat of summer. Then I acknowledged my sin to you and did not cover up my iniquity…and you forgave the guilt of my sin'.[1]

If you are harbouring guilt—real guilt, as distinct from unwarranted guilt-*feelings*— confess it, first to the Lord, who promises full forgiveness,[2] and then to the appropriate persons. Be prepared for the natural consequences. Even a term in prison is better than the awful depression caused by concealing your guilt. On the other hand, if you are not guilty of any sin, don't let the devil convince you that you are. Recognise him for the inveterate liar he is.

Involvement in the *occult*—like ouija, astrology, tarot-reading, seances, or consulting a medium—invariably produces depression. Repent of it right away, then seek expert pastoral help for the breaking of the 'strong hold' which these evil forces can exercise on the mind.

Anger and *self-pity* are also common causes. Anger may at times be justified—Jesus was sometimes angry, though always righteously so.[3] But there can never be any justification for self-pity. To put yourself at the centre through self-pity is to usurp the place of God, and that is sin. Repent of it and look for chances to serve others.

Last in this far from exhaustive list of causes of depression is *reaction to an emotional 'high'*. If you have been all keyed up over some big demand on your mental and emotional reserves such as an important examination, a wedding—especially if it is your own!—a big family celebration, giving birth (this has hormonal aspects, too), a drama production or a vital interview, an emotional 'low' is the perfectly understandable reaction.

Recognise this as normal. You don't think it unusual to be physically tired after a hard day's physical work, so why should it be unusual to be mentally tired—that is, a little depressed—after a heavy burst of mental or emotional energy?

The road to victory

It is good to be diagnosed, but better to be cured. So, in addition to the guidelines just given, what can you do to help yourself when depressed?

Start by trying to *identify the cause*. Once you have done this—and you may need some help to do it—you can begin to deal with it accordingly.

In appropriate cases *medication* may help. Normally this will be a temporary expedient. A plaster cast on a broken leg doesn't heal it; it just supports it while the healing process takes place. Antidepressant tablets are in most cases just a 'plaster cast' for the mind.

Circumstantial changes may help. If you are carrying a crippling workload, reduce it. If your normal routines of life are driving you to despair, do what you can to modify them. If circumstances permit, a holiday may help. Don't, however, make major life-changing decisions when depressed. It may seem that the circumstantial change you need is to give up your job, or leave college or seek solace in a hasty marriage, but you would probably live to regret it. Take sound pastoral advice; decisions made on your own under the stress of depression are rarely the right ones.

I mentioned above the desirability of identifying the cause of your depression. Sometimes, however, no cause will be apparent. Apart from the usual occasional 'off day', I've also known what it is to feel black despair to the point where I've understood what it is to feel suicidal. Sometimes it has been short-lived; at other times it has hung around for several months. Apart from one occasion when, through my wife's insight and wisdom, the cause was identified and dealt with, I have never been able to pinpoint any specific reason for feeling depressed. Happily, on each occasion 'it came to pass'.

Into battle!

So how should we tackle depression of this 'no obvious cause' variety?

In a word, *fight* it. All the good advice contained in the earlier chapters has been personally battle-tested by me. I have known what it is, in the sleepless small hours, to concentrate my mind on a verse of Scripture in a struggle to prevent darkness and despair from breaking in on my mind and sending me, sweating and panicking, over the brink.

I have steadfastly refused to let Satan convince me that I have no ministry just because I preached a poor sermon, or that I am a failure in general just because I have failed in some particular way.

I have known the mental struggle to keep on top of my responsibilities as a husband, father, pastor and teacher when a thousand enemy voices have clamoured 'Give up!' at the gateways of my mind.

When I have felt intense pressure to yield to weeping self-pity I have quoted to God and to the devil, but chiefly to myself, 'Be joyful always; pray continually; give thanks in all circumstances, for this is God's will for you in Christ Jesus'.[4] Then, out of dogged obedience to God, I have done just that.

At those times when a complete mental breakdown has seemed an attractive prospect, assuring me of lots of attention and the lifting off of heavy responsibilities, I have identified self-pity and self-centredness as sin and refused to give way. It would have been so very, very easy to relinquish the fight and give in.

When God has seemed a million miles away, the Bible dry and the heavens like brass, I have said to myself, 'The Lord loves me as much now as he has ever done. He is as near to me as ever, even though it doesn't feel like it at all. I won't neglect the Word, even though it seems dry just now, because it is a means of knowing my Lord better and I need to feed my mind and spirit on its teaching. Maybe my prayers do seem to bounce back from the ceiling, but I know God hears them, loves to hear them and will answer them for Jesus' sake. So I will continue to pray, and especially to worship and give thanks.'

The sun breaks through

This, then, is how to fight. Keep at it. Determine never to yield your mind to any but the Lord. 'In *him* all things hold together.'

Eventually the clouds of depression will break and disperse. The sun *will* break through. You will emerge from the experience stronger than before, your mind toughened by the exercise, equipped by it to be a sharper, more powerful instrument to serve the Lord's purpose.

And even if you have cracked under the pressure of depression, don't despair. God doesn't write you off just because you have suffered a breakdown, so don't write yourself off. Even the mighty prophet Elijah knew what it was to collapse in near-suicidal self-pity. After his triumph on Mount Carmel[5] he gave way to panic and fear, rushing away to a secluded spot where he 'prayed that he might die. "I have had enough, Lord," he said. "Take my life; I am no better than my ancestors"'.[6]

Far from writing him off, the Lord—who always looks

after his own—sent him angelic encouragement. In due course Elijah's mental and emotional balance was restored and he was off to experience new heights in his walk with the Lord and in his public ministry. It all culminated in something really special— his bodily translation directly to heaven, without seeing death. Not a bad finale for someone who, in the midst of depression, had been urging God to take his life!

If there was hope for Elijah, there is hope for you. Even if, mentally and emotionally speaking, you have touched bottom by making an attempt on your own life, God remains *for* you. The only way now is onward and upward into increasing mental stability and satisfying Christian service.

God plus one is a majority in any situation. You *can* beat depression. You can make it!

Chapter 12 NOTES

[1] Psalm 32:3-5

[2] 1 John 1:9

[3] See John 2:13-17; Mark 3:3-5

[4] 1 Thessalonians 5:16-18

[5] See 1 Kings chapter 18

[6] 1 Kings 19:4

Mind and morality

Philip listened intently, puffing on his pipe, as I gave my personal testimony to God's amazing grace. We were ensconced in a corner of the staff-room at the school where we both taught. I finished by throwing the ball into his court with, 'What's your own position, Phil, regarding God, Jesus and Christianity?'

He pondered for a moment, his eyes peering at the ceiling through the tobacco smoke.

'I think Christian morality is the highest and best any religion has to offer,' he replied, 'but to me, Christian beliefs and doctrine are just dead sticks.'

Philip was a very moral and upright man. I subsequently learned that he came from a good Methodist family, where he had been raised to practise the highest of moral standards— ones that had served him well, as Christian standards always do. People like him are becoming scarce, however. A moral legacy left by a previous generation, like a legacy of money, eventually runs out and then people have to fend for them- selves, settling their own moral standards and making their own moral decisions. Without a foundation of personal faith in Christ, the bias of their own sinful nature, coupled with the prevailing climate of ungodliness, ensures that their moral standards slip below God's ideal.

A change of mind

There is a connection between the way we think and our personal moral standards. Morality is a matter of behaviour, and behaviour, as we have seen, is governed by the way we think.

Your mind and your morality, therefore, are a married couple who refuse to be separated. Their relationship began when you made your first move towards Christ: repentance. Literally, repentance is a change of *mind* (Greek *metanoia*), and a change of mind about a moral issue at that, namely, your personal sin. When you repented you ditched your proud, self-righteous attitude and instead agreed with God that you were a sinner. Then you went on to embrace the solution he offered you in Christ.

Since that time, your mind has been undergoing renewal and, with it, so has your morality. You have been slowly discovering that 'through the fear of the Lord a man avoids evil'[1] and that 'the wisdom that comes from heaven is first of all pure'.[2]

When people reject God, the process works in reverse. If they reject him they are not going to let themselves be bound by the moral standards set out in his Book, the Bible. Their mind is therefore turned loose. Now they can think what they like and, because every human being is so constituted that he or she must have standards to live by, their mind concocts its own.

Mind and body

Self-made standards, being the product of a godless mind, are inevitably low. In his classic exposition of this question in

Romans 1:18-32, Paul stated that when people chose to reject God, 'their *thinking* became futile' and they were turned loose to follow the inclinations of 'a depraved *mind.*' The moral results of that were predictable: 'sexual impurity...the degrading of their bodies...murder...deceit' and a whole catalogue of moral decadence.

Nothing has changed since Paul's era. The same sinful principles govern human thought and behaviour today. What a radical change it is, therefore, when someone comes to faith in Christ and submits their mind to divine control. The ruts in the road are deep, however, and we shouldn't be surprised when a new believer doesn't grasp Christian moral standards all at once. One such young man said to his pastor, 'Now that I'm engaged to be married, I assume it's OK for Janet and me to sleep together?'

The pastor, a wise man, didn't raise his hands in horror. He quietly took the two of them on one side and showed them from the Word of God that sexual intercourse is only to take place within the mutual commitment of marriage. It was just one more step in the renewal of their minds and their morality, one that they took gladly out of obedience to Christ.

Conscience

The *conscience* of this young couple was being re-educated. Conscience, one of the features that marks out humankind from the animals, is closely allied to the 'peace-referee' of Colossians 3:15. The word 'conscience' literally means *'knowing with'* or *'knowing in relation to'*.

'In relation to what?' you may well ask.

In relation to your current understanding of what is right and wrong. Your conscience is like a judge in a court of law.

It examines each of your actions with the help of your current understanding of the law of God and brings a verdict. The action, or intended action, is pronounced either right or wrong. No reasons are given, and no bargaining about the verdict is allowed. Furthermore, the judgment is an individual one; *your* conscience may forbid what someone else's permits, because their understanding of right and wrong is different.

Conscience has its limitations. It was tarnished in the Fall—the event, described in Genesis 3, that marked the entry of sin into human experience. Like an old mirror whose silvering is flaked and surface cracked, conscience remains of some use, but it gives a far from perfect representation of the will of God.

We could liken conscience to a compass. When I go hill-walking I always take a compass. But I also take a map, because the compass is of limited value on its own. As Christians, our map is the Bible, but those who either don't have the Bible or don't recognise its authority still carry the mental compass. Not surprisingly, it proves of limited value.

Learning the hard way

As a student I spent several months in Spain. On one occasion, in the centre of Madrid, I decided to buy a newspaper. Spotting a newspaper kiosk at the other side of the busy street, I waited for a gap in the traffic and nipped across.

Just as I was handing over my money and taking the paper, a heavy hand fell upon my shoulder. It was a traffic policeman, who informed me that I had broken the local by-laws by crossing where I did and that I would have to pay an on-the-spot fine. My plea of ignorance fell on deaf ears. Mercifully, the fine was very small!

The point is that I felt no conscience about crossing the street where I did because I was totally ignorant of the Madrid by-law stating that in the city centre one was permitted to cross the street only at crossings with traffic lights. Once I knew the law, however, my conscience began to operate on that basis.

Our conscience can be moulded by a variety of factors. *Tradition* is a powerful one: a non-Christian may say, 'I'd feel terrible if I didn't go to church for the midnight service on Christmas Eve' simply because she was brought up that way.

Current social attitudes are another factor. As a result of animal rights activity, lots of people today, for instance, would feel guilty about wearing a genuine fur coat, though they would happily wear one made of leather or sheepskin.

Our *parents* instil standards into us. Fred is about to clean his shoes. He spreads a newspaper on the table and puts his shoes on it, only to have a twinge of conscience based on a childhood memory: his superstitious mother's words, 'It brings bad luck to put shoes on the table.'

Conscience can be partly deadened or desensitised by drugs, alcohol or even endless work. Paul writes about 'hypocritical liars, whose consciences have been seared as with a hot iron'.[3] Just as branding with a hot iron damages the nerves in the skin to produce desensitised scar-tissue, a person's conscience can be desensitised by persistent wickedness so that they seem able to commit the vilest of atrocities without any apparent sense of guilt.

Conscience re-educated

When you became a Christian things began to change in this respect. With God's law now being written on your heart by his Holy Spirit, your conscience became more sensitive to right and wrong. The compass became a much more reliable guide for living by being used along with the map of God's Word. The inner judge was now able to make pronouncements about your actions on the basis, not of any old book, but of *the* Book.

Your conscience is being re-educated as you soak your mind in Scripture. You may have once felt guilty about keeping your eyes open during prayer, but realising now that the Bible lays down no 'eyes closed' rule, you feel free to keep them open when appropriate. Pangs of guilt about eating a pork chop disappear in the light of the Bible's clear statement that, 'No food is unclean in itself...all food is clean'.[4] While the principle of one day's rest in seven remains a sound guide to health, your fears about being struck by a thunderbolt for buying an ice cream on a Sunday will vanish when you understand that the observing of special 'religious' days is mere legalism.[5]

This re-education of the conscience, being part of the renewing of the mind, takes time. It is another 'ruts in the road' process. In the meantime, live according to its present dictates, following Paul's teaching that 'each one should be fully convinced *in his own mind*'.[6]

Intellectualism and morality

It would be helpful at this stage to note the poverty of intellectualism when it comes to settling moral issues. Is it mere coincidence that student life is marked by so much moral confusion and sexual immorality?

'The reason for much poverty of thought,' noted Watchman Nee, 'lies in thinking too much.' That is the intellectual's problem. Just as a blind man compensates for his handicap by developing his sense of hearing, smell, taste and touch to an unusually high degree, the person devoid of *spiritual* life will focus on developing his powers of *mind* or *body*. The body-conscious may go in for physical culture, becoming obsessed with health and fitness, or he may indulge his physical appetites on the basis of 'Eat, drink and be merry, for tomorrow we die'—a fine example of godless philosophy.

The more intellectually inclined person—the mind-conscious—may pursue research into some abstruse area of study or try to navigate the notoriously unpredictable waters of philosophy or psychology. Though he may claim to be an agnostic, or even an atheist, he will in fact acknowledge some god. He will worship at the shrine of 'ideas', 'humanism', 'pure thought' or 'science'.

But the spiritual person holds the key to the whole of life. His mind is liberated through submission to God. His body is cared for and respected as nothing less than the temple of the Holy Spirit. He alone knows the blessing of Christian morality. He is truly a whole person.

The gospel for the intellectual

An evangelistic mission on a university campus attracted little interest among the students until a notice appeared stating that the topic of Thursday's talk would be 'The Gospel for the Intellectual'. Large numbers of 'intellectuals' turned up, only to hear that the gospel for the intellectual was, 'You must be born again'.

The speaker talked about a Bible intellectual named Nicodemus whose encounter with Jesus is recorded in John chapter three. Nicodemus tried to explore spiritual dimensions with human logic—as fruitless an enterprise as trying to do brain surgery with a spade. In the end, Jesus explained that the only way to tackle the vital question of his relationship with God was on a spiritual basis—through repentance and faith. Mind had to bow to divine revelation.

Nothing has changed since Nicodemus's day. The philosophy that so delights the mind of the intellectual is still branded 'hollow and deceptive' by the spiritual person,[7] who will remain wary of 'what is falsely called knowledge'.[8] The gospel for the intellectual is still, 'You must be born again.'

Intellectualism has always been heavy on questions but light on answers. It stirs up a lot of dust, only to complain that it can't see. In fact, when it comes to facing life's deepest issues, the inability to 'see' truth has become such a feature of the intellectual that he has given up trying to see and has elevated blindness to the status of a virtue. He honours doubt, and despises conviction and certainty as the follies of the intellectually underdeveloped. He thinks shivering in 'the draft from an open mind' is something to be proud of.

In pubs and university common rooms, social clubs and debating societies one can find people enjoying a good discussion on some aspect of religion, morality or politics. But at the end of it all no decision is reached; everyone takes it for granted that there can be no final answer to these questions. They didn't enter the discussion expecting to find answers; they joined in simply to enjoy the thrust and parry, the back and forth, the give and take of a good argument. Without Christ they are 'always learning but *never able to acknowledge the truth'.*[9]

Settled convictions

But Christians have reached some settled convictions by submitting their minds to the revelation of God. Rejecting Stevenson's dictum that 'To travel hopefully is better than to arrive', they have 'arrived' at certain conclusions about life and morality which, far from spoiling the fun, have provided a basis for truly pleasurable living.

Comparing Timothy's happy position with that of the godless intellectuals mentioned above, Paul declares, 'But as for you, continue in what you have learned and have *become convinced of*.[10] As Christians we have solid, Bible-based convictions on such crucial areas as marriage, the raising of children, abortion, euthanasia, death, suicide, sex, divorce and crime and punishment.

Convictions are essential if we are to live with any degree of peace of mind. When in doubt, we ask, 'What does *God* say?' Where he makes a clear statement, we accept it without question. Where he doesn't, we apply the broad principles of God-revealed wisdom with the help of the Holy Spirit and so reach a practical conclusion.

Burdens rightly shared

A hill-walker was introducing his six-year-old son to the delights of the hills. The small boy, filled with excitement, insisted on carrying everything—the map and compass, the whistle, the survival bag, the flask of hot coffee, the sandwiches, the extra sweaters, the first-aid kit, the spare socks and everything else.

After a quarter of a mile he asked his dad to take the heavy sweaters and flask. A few hundred yards further on he passed over the first-aid kit. Soon, the map hanging round his neck in its plastic case was chafing his skin. This, too, was given to Dad. Gradually, the little boy parted with everything except his own tiny rucksack with his sandwich and apple in it.

'Now I can really enjoy the walk,' he remarked. And he did. Dad, being used to a heavy rucksack, was well able to carry the rest.

The non-Christian intellectual carries on his own shoulders the crippling weight of the countless moral decisions that have to be made in the course of life's journey. Sadly, he has no 'Dad' to refer them to, which is why he doesn't enjoy the walk. Only God's shoulders are broad enough to bear the weight of deciding what is right and wrong. He is delighted to relieve his children of the heavy burden, thereby freeing them to enjoy life's journey to the full.

'Prepare your minds for action,' says Peter.[11] An athlete goes into action stripped of every unnecessary weight. As we pass on to God these mental weights that only he is fitted to carry, our minds are prepared to go into action with every hope of success.

True intellectual freedom

Far from being an intellectual dwarf, the child of God knows what intellectual growth really means because his mind is free. He has discovered that true freedom lies, not in doing one's own thing, but in having the right Master. Under the control of God, his mind has been liberated to a degree unknown to the unbeliever with even the highest IQ, and he can turn his sharpened intelligence to the pursuit of true knowledge and science.

While the powerful locomotive of the unbeliever's mind is

quickly derailed and bogged down in the nearest intellectual and moral quagmire, the mind of the Christian truly goes places. Restricted, as it is, to the rails of God's revelation, its immense power is liberated to carry mental freight to destinations at the very frontiers of human knowledge.

Far from being 'out of this world', the Christian is the only one truly in control of it, because only the person *under* authority is equipped to be *in* authority.

Unlike the atheistic intellectual who, being his own king, is incapable of rule and is destined to end up in intellectual and moral turmoil, the Christian bows the knee to King Jesus, and in so doing is invested with the vice-regency of the created order. Under Christ he exercises true dominion, marking the physical, mental, emotional and moral aspects of earthly life with the stamp of divine order.

Have you noticed something? We keep coming back to the same thing: submit your mind to God.

Now move on from there. Educate your conscience according to his Word. Let him guide your moral decisions. Let him thus liberate your mind for action.

Chapter 13 NOTES

[1] Proverbs 16:6

[2] James 3:17

[3] 1 Timothy 4:2

[4] Romans 14:14, 20; see also Mark 7:19

[5] See Galatians 4:9-10; Colossians 2:16-17

[6] Romans 14:5

[7] Colossians 2:8

Prepare for action!

Reading this book will be a complete waste of time if, at the end, it doesn't lead you to take some action. Hence the title of this final chapter.

Already we have come across Peter's command: 'Prepare your minds for action'.[1] In the old King James Version it reads, more literally, 'Gird up the loins of your mind.'

This expression, meaningless to most English-speaking people today, is a reference to Eastern culture. In Bible days, everyday robes were worn down to the ankles, which made it very awkward when it came to hard physical work. The free movement of legs and thighs was hindered. When a man prepared for work, therefore, he would 'gird up his loins'. That is, he would hitch up the skirts of his clothing and tuck them into his belt, leaving his legs free.

That is exactly what we have to do with our minds: pull away every hindrance and so free them for *action*. So let's review the substance of the previous chapters, focusing on what you can *do* now to help yourself.

A plan of action

1. Embrace the fact that a sound mind is your birthright as a Christian. Accept that Paul's statement about Jesus—'In him all things hold together'—includes your mind.

Say: 'I gratefully accept, Lord, the mental stability that you have guaranteed to those who love you. Help me to live out the implications of it, in accordance with your Word.'

2. Depose King Reason from the throne and acknowledge God as the rightful ruler over your thinking. *Let* him govern your mind. Submit your mind to his Word and to his Holy Spirit.

   Say: 'Lord, I gladly acknowledge your rule over my mind. Help me to appreciate that the restrictions placed on my thinking by your Spirit and your Word are for my blessing.'

3. Accept the responsibility that he hands back to you for the day-to-day running of your thinking. Face up to the fact that you can, and must, choose what you think about.

   Say: 'From now on I refuse to let my thoughts run rampage like undisciplined children. I hereby take them in hand and bring the discipline of God into my thinking. No thought will remain independent; every one will now be allowed to act only under my jurisdiction.'

4. Become the immigration officer at the gateways to your mind—Eye Gate, Ear Gate, Memory Gate and Habit Gate—and be as ruthless in denying entry to unhelpful thoughts as you are warm in welcoming positive ones.

   Say: 'Since government and peace go hand in hand,[2] I will bring peace to my mind by enforcing upon would-be-immigrant thoughts the strict checks that my Lord demands. Only those carrying the passport of his approval will be permitted to enter.'

5. If necessary, seek help in the initial pulling down of any strongholds that the enemy may have established in your mind.

   Say: 'Lord, please show me if there are outposts of enemy control anywhere in my mind, so that I can call for help to rid my mind of them for ever and so bring *every* thought into captivity to Christ.'

6. Once a stronghold has been demolished, maintain godly standards of thinking 'in keeping with' that victory, refusing to let your mind slip back permanently into the old ruts.

   Say: 'Save me, Lord, from the naïve notion that initial victory in my thought life is automatically permanent. Remind me, by your Holy Spirit, of the need to keep acting in line with your takeover plan.'

7. Remembering the danger of a mental vacuum, actively fill your mind with thoughts of whatever is true, noble, right, pure, lovely, admirable, excellent and praiseworthy. Open a bank account of quality thoughts.

   Say: 'Thank you, Lord, for providing so much good food for thought. Thank you for an endless supply of wholesome and nourishing material to build up a healthy mind.'

8. Feed your mind on the Word of God. Let it flow through it to 'wash the wool'. Begin a programme of regular Bible reading, or listen to it on CD. Meditate on the Bible, learning sections of it by heart, so that the Holy Spirit can bring appropriate verses to mind in times of need.

   Say: 'I have hidden your word in my heart that I might not sin against you'.[3]

9. Be transformed from the inside out—metamorphosed like the caterpillar to the butterfly—by the renewing of your mind. Co-operate with God by 'working out' what he is 'working in' you. Bring the silver of godliness to the surface.

    Say: 'I won't wait until Christ returns before I change; by the renewing of my mind I will begin to change here and now.'

10. Give close attention to the kind of films you watch on the screen of your imagination, remembering that what you see there will mould your character and your destiny. Become a film producer. Star in films which portray you as the child of God that you in fact are.

    Say: 'I am a success, a person of unique value and worth, created in Christ Jesus to be a blessing wherever I go, and that's how I will envisage myself.'

11. Doggedly refuse to give way to anxiety. Instead, wield the weapons of thanksgiving and prayer. That way, the peace of God will guard your heart and mind in Christ Jesus.

    Say: 'I will not be eaten away by worry. God is my Father. He has all things in control. I will act wisely and responsibly at all times and leave with Father the working out of the circumstances that are beyond my own control.'

12. Tackle every decision in the conviction that you can get it right. Survey the options open to you; remember that there will probably not be one perfect course to take; seek advice; listen to the 'peace referee'. Then choose and act. Ignore subsequent doubts.

    Say: 'Lord, you are decisive and I, as your child, intend to be the same. A wrong decision is better than no decision, because I can learn from it. But with your help, Lord, I aim to make wise decisions every time.'

13. Determine to beat depression. Take the appropriate steps to deal with root causes, then simply fight it. Accept medication where appropriate. Refuse to go under.

   Say: 'Thank you, Lord, that you won't let me be tested beyond what I can bear and that you will enable me to stand up under the weight of depression.[4] I will fight, and I will win. Satan will never again score a victory here.'

14. Allow your moral standards to be governed by the Word of God. Re-educate your conscience in accordance with Scripture so that you regularly use 'map' and 'compass' together.

   Say: 'I praise you, Lord, for the solid foundation of moral conviction that you have provided for me in your Word. I will walk confidently and uprightly, unsnared by either legalism or licentiousness.'

15. Reject the humanist philosophy that makes doubt and uncertainty a virtue. Instead, rejoice to know that by letting God decide the limits of your thinking, your mind, far from being stifled, is truly set free.

   Say: 'Thank you for showing me, Lord, that true freedom lies in having the right Master. My mind, by being bound to your will and your Word, is truly free. Enable me, Lord, to use it for your glory.'

Chapter 14 NOTES

[1] 1 Peter 1:13

[2] See Isaiah 9:7

[3] Psalm 119:11

[4] 1 Corinthians 10:13

Becoming a Christian

If some parts of this book have made good sense to you while the more 'religious' bits have seemed like gobbledygook, you have come to the right place. Read on.

By 'Christian' I don't mean 'goes to church' or 'got christened as a baby' or 'pops into cathedrals now and again to hedge his bets by lighting a candle.' I'm talking about what the Bible—which is God's Word—says on the subject. You yourself might not yet believe it is God's Word, but read on anyway; it can't do you any harm and your condition is curable.

Who God is

God exists, all-powerful and all-loving. He is a living, eternal Spirit who created everything and sustains it by his power. He is not the same thing as the universe but exists separately from it. Nor is he just another word for the 'inner self', discoverable by looking within ourselves. God is certainly interested in your 'inner self', as we have seen earlier in this book, but he himself exists outside of you.

God is what Christians call a 'Trinity'—one God but existing in three distinct 'persons': Father, Son and Holy Spirit. That is important. It means that, at the very heart of what God is, is relationship. What is more, the relationship that God enjoyed within the Trinity from eternity past he now delights to extend to human beings. To know God this way is the summit of human fulfilment.

There is a problem, however, in our achieving that relationship, because the world and its inhabitants are all smitten with a spiritual and moral disease that the Bible calls 'sin'. So not only are we unable to reach God because of the immense 'size gap' between us as creatures and himself as the Creator, but also by the 'sin gap', which is even greater. God is infinitely good, holy, right and pure, and alongside him we are impossibly dirty.

Not that we particularly *want* to reach out to God. Most of the time our natural sinful condition inclines us to ignore him and do our own thing. That means that if there is ever going to be any reconciliation between God and ourselves, God himself will have to take the initiative to bridge the gaps.

This he has done. Good news!

How God has broken in

God has broken in in two ways. First, over the centuries he has broken into the lives of individuals like Noah, Abraham and Moses, and later into the life of a nation, ancient Israel, to whom he spoke through their prophets. He thus revealed himself in manageable stages—manageable by us, that is— and the whole process was recorded in what we now call the Old Testament, the first of the two major sections of the Bible.

The main theme of the Old Testament is the promise of the eventual arrival of one called the Messiah, who would complete the process of God's revelation of himself to a lost and confused humanity.

That Messiah was Jesus Christ who, as the second

'person' of the Trinity, was himself divine. The other major section of the Bible—the New Testament—records his arrival among us and its exciting consequences.

Jesus: who he is and what he did

Jesus, the eternal Son of God, 'took flesh' and came among us as a real man. He was born supernaturally to a virgin, Mary, and lived a life of moral perfection. Tempted just like you and me, he never yielded once; he never sinned.

At the age of thirty he embarked on three years of public service, moving around the Holy Land teaching, healing the sick and, most unexpectedly, warning of his imminent premature death. That death, he indicated, would have greater consequences than even his sinless life, for somehow it would 'finish the job' of opening the door for sinful human beings to be reconciled to the holy God whom he called his 'Father'.

The Jewish and Roman authorities in due course combined to put him to death by crucifixion, which is why the cross has become a symbol of Christian faith. He died for us, that is, he took our place because we, being sinners, were the ones who deserved to die.

But then—wait for it!—three days later he came alive again, not in some spooky 'spiritual' way but in a literal sense. After this resurrection he had a physical body that his followers instantly recognised, yet it now had super-human powers, like being able to pass through locked doors. The risen Jesus spent six weeks with his followers, talking about the kingdom of God that he was soon to inaugurate.

Then he left them and ascended to heaven. Shortly after, he poured out the Holy Spirit on his waiting disciples. This was an overwhelming supernatural experience that filled them with joy, with boldness in telling others about Jesus, and with supernatural gifts like 'speaking in tongues' and prophesying.

This began a whole new era in God's dealings with humanity. Thanks to what Jesus had achieved, the door was now open for all who believed to be reconciled to God and enjoy a real relationship with him—one that would grow in depth and intensity throughout life. And after that, death would bring them into the presence of the Lord they loved, to await the final triumph: his return to earth in power and glory.

That event is still future. When it happens, he will wind up the affairs of this sad old world and put a final end to sin, sorrow, pain, tears and sickness, after which his people will enjoy his presence in unspeakable joy and fulfilment for all eternity.

Getting into the good of it

The key question now is: how do you get into this relationship with God that Jesus came to make possible? The fact that you are reading this at all means that God is probably on your case already, drawing you to himself, so in what way should you respond?

The Bible outlines four steps that begin the amazing journey of the Christian life.

The first is to *repent*.

This old-fashioned-sounding word means to agree with God's verdict about your sinfulness, in other words, to admit that you fall far short of God's requirements and have no hope at all of earning his approval.

'Well, of course nobody's perfect,' you say.

Quite right, but that is not the point. You may well be a

better person than many—more upright, more helpful, more generous with your giving to the needy and so on. But that's like one person saying to another, 'I can jump higher than you' when you only get a prize if you can jump high enough to touch the moon. Jumping two metres off the ground beats jumping only twenty centimetres, but it is nowhere near moon-touching.

God's standard is perfection, and you have failed to meet it—by a million miles. Repenting means accepting the fact that you have sinned, and then doing something about it. It means facing up to specific sins: bitterness towards a relative; stealing office stationery; indulging in casual sex; lying; blowing your own trumpet, or whatever. What is more, it means making up your mind to stop. You may have tried and failed time and time again, but this time you will cry out to God, 'God, I can't do it on my own. Help me, please!' He will.

The second step is to *believe in Jesus.*

Not just believing that he existed, or that he was a great prophet, or even that he was the Son of God, all of which are true. No, in particular it means believing that if you are ever to have the relationship with God that you both need and want, it will be because Jesus, through his death for you, made it available to you as a gift.

Note the word 'gift'. That is a key factor. Most of us don't like accepting charity in any form; we prefer to maintain our pride by making some sort of payment or contribution. But God has made it absolutely clear that we cannot do that. He doesn't 'sell' anything, least of all admittance to a relationship with himself. He offers it only as a free gift, on the strength of what Jesus has done through his sinless life, his death for you and his resurrection.

Believing in Jesus, then, means coming to God with the empty hands of faith and saying, 'God, my hands are empty. I've nothing to offer you in even part-payment for your great salvation. I'm far from good enough, but Jesus was and is more than good enough, so I am throwing myself on your mercy, God, and asking you to accept me, not for my own sake, but for his.'

God always says yes to that request when it comes from a sincere heart.

The third step is to submit to *baptism.*

This is the Bible way by which you affirm—to God, to yourself and to your friends and relatives—that you have said goodbye to your old self-centred life and now intend to live entirely for God.

Biblical baptism means being immersed fully under the water of a river, pool or baptismal tank in the presence of witnesses. Normally a church leader would carry this out. It is a wonderful, very physical experience that you will never forget. And when later you go through tough times you can look back to your baptism and remind yourself, 'I did it in good faith, and I meant it. In doing it I signalled my determination to live God's way from that point on, and that's what, with his continued help, I'm going to carry on doing.'

The fourth and final step that starts you on the Christian pathway is being *baptised in the Holy Spirit.*

This is the Lord's response to your act of submitting to baptism in water. You allowed yourself to be immersed in the water; now he responds by immersing you in the Holy Spirit. This is a wonderfully overwhelming experience of God's closeness, power and presence that will probably leave you lost for words as to how to thank and praise God enough for his love to you. Indeed, you may well find yourself bursting out in strange sounds, like some foreign language. This is called 'speaking in tongues' and is normal in these circumstances.

These four steps may take place in close succession, maybe even all the same day, or maybe over a period of days, weeks or even months. The timing and the order of the steps will vary because we all have a unique background and experience and God touches us accordingly in different ways. But, one way or another, it's these four steps that get you started on the Christian path. It is is this way that you are reconciled to God, become his true child and join his great family.

Living as God's child

That is not the end, of course; it is just the beginning. The path winds into the future. It takes you from day to day in a wonderful living relationship with God as your Father, with Jesus as your Friend and Brother, and with the Holy Spirit as your Guide and Counsellor living right inside you.

When this is your experience—and I pray it will indeed be—you will be able to read this book again and find, to your amazement and joy, that the 'religious' bits are the best bits of all.

About the author

David Matthew was born in 1940. He was raised in a Christian family active among the Open Brethren. He became a committed Christian himself at the age of twelve.

After gaining a degree in Spanish and French and a Post-Graduate Certificate in Education he taught at schools in the city of Bradford, England, for thirteen years, before entering the Christian ministry in the emerging 'new church' scene in Bradford.

In 1980 David moved out of his pastoral role to set up a Bible college for Covenant Ministries, the ministry team led by the late Bryn Jones, both teaching and serving as Principal for some years. Later, he was editor of the team's magazine, *Restoration,* for eight years and began writing books, as well as editing a multi-volume body of theological material, Covenant College's *Modular Training Programme,* for use in the college's distance-learning curriculum.

The years 1996-7 saw him in South Africa, once again establishing a Bible college for a network of churches there.

Since his return to the UK in 1998 he has been part of the eldership team of Five Towns Christian Fellowship, Castleford, where his chief role is teaching the Scriptures. He also travels regularly to teach in other churches both in Britain and overseas.

David is married to Faith and they have three grown-up children.